SEASONAL GUIDE TO THE NATURAL YEAR

Seasonal Guide to the Natural Year

A Month by Month Guide to Natural Events

Texas

Steve Price

Fulcrum Publishing
Golden, Colorado

The Seasonal Guide to the Natural Year Series

Pennsylvania, New Jersey, Maryland, Delaware, Virginia, West Virginia and Washington, D.C., Scott Weidensaul

New England and New York, Scott Weidensaul

Illinois, Missouri and Arkansas, Barbara Perry Lawton

Colorado, New Mexico, Arizona and Utah, Ben Guterson

Northern California, Bill McMillon

Oregon, Washington and British Columbia, James Luther Davis

Texas, Steve Price

Forthcoming Titles

North Carolina, South Carolina and Tennessee, John Rucker

Florida with Georgia and Alabama Coasts, M. Timothy O'Keefe

Minnesota, Michigan and Wisconsin, John Bates

Southern California, Judy Wade

Book design by Deborah Rich
Cover photograph of Cerro Castellan Peak in Big Bend National Park
copyright © 1996 Tom Till
Interior photographs by Steve Price.

Library of Congress Cataloging-in-Publication Data

Price, Steve.
Seasonal guide to the natural year : a month by month guide to natural events. Texas / Steve Price.
p. cm.
Includes bibliographical references and index.
ISBN 1-55591-272-9 (pbk.)
1. Natural history—Texas—Guidebooks. 2. Seasons—Texas—Guidebooks. 3. Texas—Guidebooks. I. Title
QH105.T4P75 1996
575.9764—dc20 96-5270
CIP

Maps included in this book are for general reference only. For more detailed maps and additional information, contact the agencies or specific sites listed in the appendix.

Printed in the United States of America

0 9 8 7 6 5 4 3 2 1

Fulcrum Publishing
350 Indiana Street, Suite 350
Golden, Colorado 80401-5093
(800) 992-2908 • (303) 277-1623

This book is dedicated to the memory of the late Byron W. Dalrymple of Kerrville, Texas, who opened the door for a young writer so many years ago; and to Patti and Buck, who keep it open today.

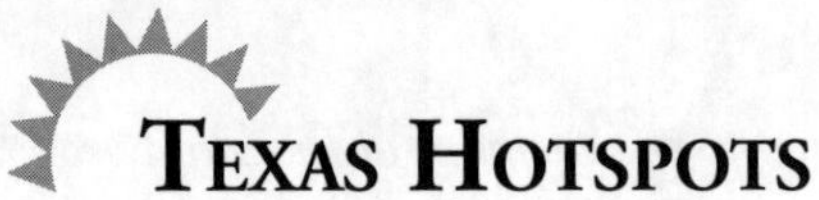

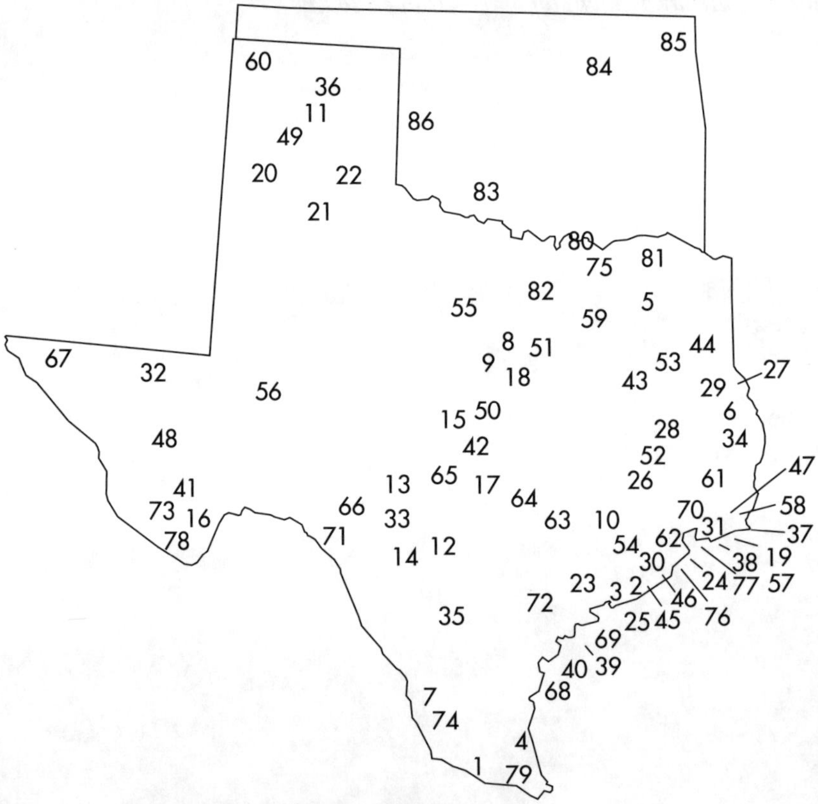

Seasonal Guide to the Natural Year

Site Locator Map

N

List of Sites

Texas

1. Bentsen–Rio Grande Valley State Park
2. Aransas National Wildlife Refuge
3. Little Bay and the Connie Hagar Wildlife Sanctuary
4. Laguna Atascosa National Wildlife Refuge
5. Lake Fork
6. Sam Rayburn Reservoir
7. Lake Falcon
8. Dinosaur Valley State Park
9. Fossil Rim Wildlife Center
10. Attwater Prairie Chicken National Wildlife Refuge
11. Palo Duro Canyon State Park
12. Kerr Wildlife Management Area
13. South Llano River State Park
14. Hill Country State Natural Area
15. Colorado Bend State Park
16. Big Bend National Park
17. Pedernales Falls State Park
18. Meridian State Park
19. Sea Rim State Park
20. Muleshoe National Wildlife Refuge
21. Mackenzie State Park
22. Caprock Canyons State Park
23. Welder Wildlife Refuge
24. Galveston Island State Park
25. Rockport-Fulton Demonstration Garden
26. Sam Houston National Forest
27. Sabine National Forest
28. Davy Crockett National Forest
29. Angelina National Forest
30. Brazos Bend State Park
31. Armand Bayou Nature Center
32. Guadalupe Mountains National Park
33. Lost Maples State Natural Area
34. Martin Dies Jr. State Park
35. Choke Canyon State Park
36. Lake Meredith National Recreation Area
37. Texas Point National Wildlife Refuge
38. Bolivar Peninsula/Bolivar Flats Shorebird Sanctuary
39. Goose Island State Park
40. Padre Island National Seashore
41. Elephant Mountain Wildlife Management Area
42. Inks Lake State Park
43. Fairfield Lake State Park
44. Martin Creek Lake State Park
45. San Bernard National Wildlife Refuge
46. Brazoria National Wildlife Refuge
47. Anahuac National Wildlife Refuge
48. Davis Mountains State Park
49. Buffalo Lake National Wildlife Refuge
50. Lake Buchanan
51. Brazos River
52. Trinity River
53. Lake o' the Pines

54. Eagle Lake
55. Possum Kingdom State Park
56. Monahans Sandhills State Park
57. High Island
58. Sabine Woods
59. Great Trinity Forest
60. Rita Blanca National Grasslands
61. Big Thicket National Preserve
62. Big Reef Nature Park
63. Bastrop State Park
64. Congress Avenue Bridge
65. Old Tunnel Wildlife Management Area
66. Kickapoo Cavern State Park
67. Franklin Mountains State Park
68. Mustang Island State Park
69. Matagorda Island State Park
70. Mercer Arboretum
71. Seminole Canyon State Park
72. King Ranch
73. Big Bend Ranch State Park
74. Falcon State Park
75. Hagerman National Wildlife Refuge
76. San Luis Pass
77. Pelican Island
78. El Camino del Rio
79. Santa Ana National Wildlife Refuge
80. Lake Texoma
81. Caddo National Grassland
82. LBJ National Grassland

List of Sites

Oklahoma

83. Wichita Mountains National Wildlife Refuge
84. Tallgrass Prairie Preserve
85. Grand Lake of the Cherokees
86. Black Kettle National Grassland

Contents

Acknowledgments

By their very design, travel books require input and assistance from many different sources, and this volume is certainly no exception. In fact, because it involves not only travel but also the vast world of wildlife and nature, it probably required even more such input.

Naming each of the individuals who contributed their advice, suggestions, and directions would fill a volume of its own, so I offer only blanket thanks to the agencies those individuals represent. First and foremost are the personnel of the Texas Parks and Wildlife Department, most of whom never realized they were being quizzed by a book author. In every instance, however, the biologists, technicians, and park personnel assisted in every manner possible. They were truly refreshing to work with and certainly made my job much easier.

The same holds true for the many people I spoke to in the U.S. Fish and Wildlife Service. Harried as they always were, each did his or her best to satisfy my informational requirements. Likewise, the Southwest Regional Office of the National Audubon Society provided prompt help and advice with each telephone call I made to it, and there were many.

Finally, chambers of commerce and visitor and convention bureaus throughout Texas must also receive a nod of thanks for their help. I now have boxes of maps and brochures as a testimony of their diligence. I enjoyed reading them the first time around, and I'm sure I'll enjoy them further in the years to come.

Introduction

Anyone who lives in Texas, has ever visited the state, or perhaps has only looked at it on a map quickly realizes one undeniable fact: It's a big place. Roughly 800 miles apart from north to south or east to west, its boundaries embrace more than 267,000 square miles. It is actually farther from Texarkana to El Paso than it is from Los Angeles to El Paso.

In the natural world, this size translates into a unique meeting ground of several distinct ecological zones, which in turn explain the Lone Star State's incredible diversity of fauna and flora. This is literally where north meets south and east meets west, resulting not only in plants and animals unique to Texas but in entire ecosystems unique to the state.

These plants and animals and ecosystems do not live by a human clock but by nature's clock. Birds migrate, whitetail deer grow their antlers, bluebonnets bloom not on our schedule but on theirs, and they do it pretty predictably. Something is happening every month—every week and every day, actually—of the year, and that is what this book is about.

Seasonal Guide to the Natural Year: Texas is a guidebook with a dual purpose. The first is to describe when these different events take place and where to see them as they happen. In every instance, the locations pinpointed are public places, such as state parks or national refuges. Not every potential viewing site has been listed, because the book would then become nothing more than a listing and its second purpose would be lost.

That second purpose is to make each reader aware of the unequaled splendor of the natural world that is available for all to see every week from one corner of the state to another. With that increased awareness, hopefully, will come an increased feeling of stewardship for the land and the creatures that use it. Even after a century of studying bird migrations we don't fully understand them, but that does not stop us from enjoying their majesty and their mystery.

Stop to think for a moment, however, of a world without those migrations. To that end, several bird-nesting sites along the coast have been deemed too fragile for inclusion in this book, and indeed, much of Big Bend Ranch State Park's nearly 300,000 acres is still closed to the public for the same reason.

The best way to enjoy any of the natural events described in this book is to do it on nature's terms. That means not only being in the right place at the right time but also respecting the beauty of the event for its own sake.

In *Seasonal Guide to the Natural Year: Texas,* each month has six chapters. Four chapters describe major viewing and activity opportunities and include a brief natural history as well as suggested "hot spots" for viewing. Each "Shorttakes" chapter focuses more briefly on an additional viewing opportunity, while the "Closer Look" chapters describe certain plant or animal species in more general terms without specific viewing spots.

Once you begin traveling in Texas, you will quickly see its diversity. No single state offers as much within its borders, which is what makes nature study in Texas so interesting. There is something new and exciting at each turn of the road, and, hopefully, this book will help you discover it.

General Tips, Cautions, and Suggestions

If the gold is truly in the going, as they say, then one way to make each trip more golden is by preparing in advance. The chapters in this book give brief descriptions of events in the natural world; if something truly interests you, spend the time to study it further. All the places listed in this book have brochures and other information available, and additional information can certainly be obtained from local libraries.

One of the first booklets every traveler should consider purchasing is *The Roads of Texas* atlas, which includes more than 50 pages of interstate, state, county, and park roads. Far more detailed than an ordinary road map, the atlas will not only help you get to the sites listed in this book but will also open up the state for your own personal exploration. It is available in bookstores statewide.

Although every precaution has been taken to list road numbers correctly in this book, some may have been changed between the time of writing and when you read this book. When you're planning your trip, double check road numbers and directions with current road maps or by telephone.

Because each Texas state park charges a daily entrance fee, purchasing the Texas Conservation Passport is definitely advisable for frequent travelers. At $25, it provides reduced fees at all state parks for a full 12 months. It's available at all state parks.

Remember, also, that a number of the species listed in this book are legal game animals for hunting, and hunting is a very important activity across the state. Certain areas may be closed or otherwise restricted during hunting season, so plan your visit accordingly.

A final word of caution regarding the weather. Texans, like the people of many states in the Southwest, are fond of noting that the weather here changes every five minutes. While that may be stretching the truth a little, Texas weather certainly can change in a hurry, especially in the spring and fall. Make sure you're prepared.

The same weather changes can also affect plant and animal timetables and behavior. If you have questions about a specific event, telephone ahead. See the appendix for a list of addresses and phone numbers.

January

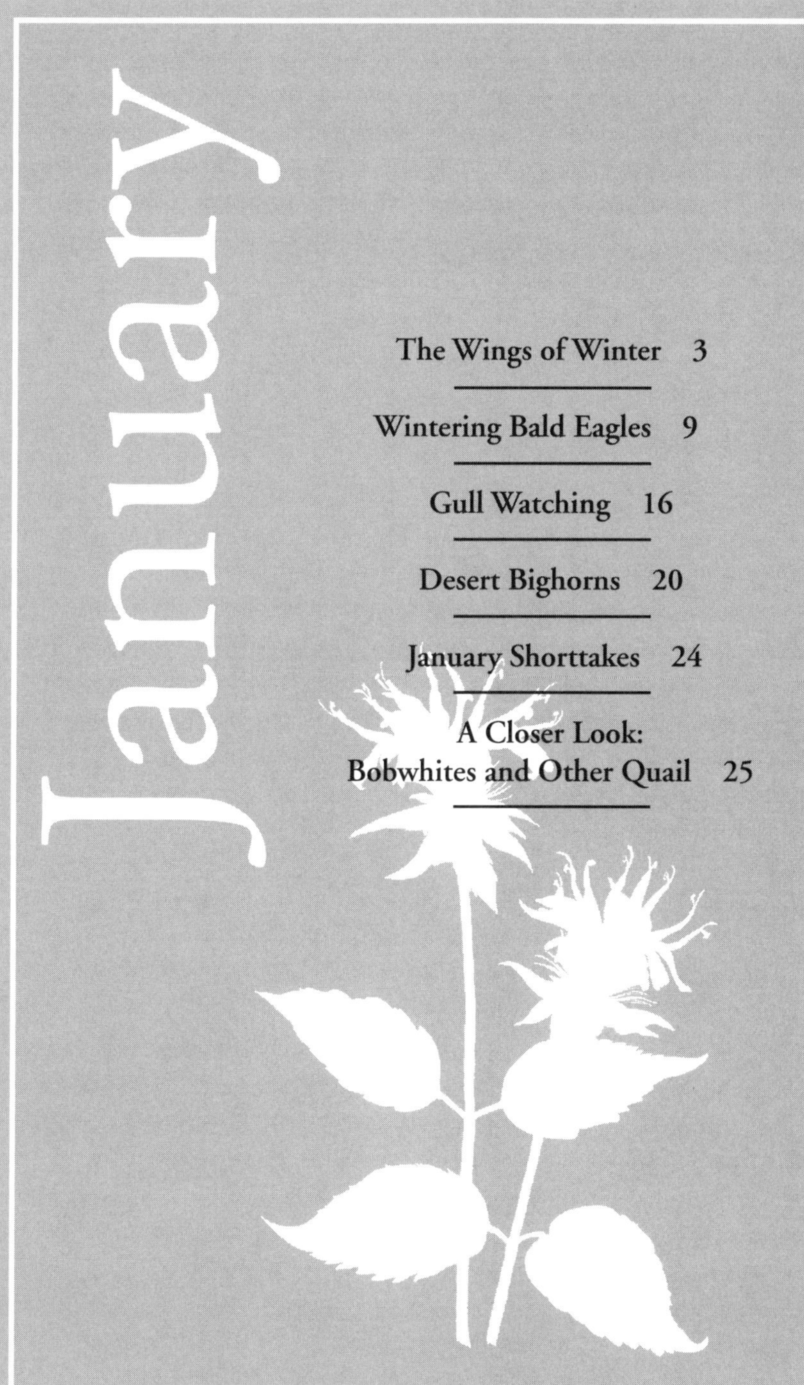

Notes

1

The Wings of Winter

Purists may lament that all the world's great mysteries have been solved, for, after all, the Pyramids have been opened, the battlefield of Troy excavated, even the moon has been explored. Everest has been scaled, the Amazon navigated, and Antarctica mapped.

For naturalists, however, one mystery that has puzzled humankind for thousands of years still cannot be completely explained. It is the mystery of bird migration, the twice-annual movement of hundreds of species from summer nesting grounds to warm wintering areas and back again.

Texas is one of the greatest benefactors of the fall migration, as literally hundreds of thousands of birds come from their summer homes as far away as the Canadian Arctic to spend several warm months along the state's 380 miles of Gulf coast and nearby brush and woodland habitats.

In its broadest sense, bird migration is simply an effort to seek out a more favorable habitat, to avoid the severe conditions of winter, and to find adequate food supplies. Nevertheless, this does not begin to explain how birds know when to migrate, since not all species follow the same timetable; nor does it answer how birds navigate and find the very same wintering spots year after year.

Bird migrations were observed nearly 3,000 years ago by Aristotle, Homer, and other Greek philosophers, and there are several biblical references to bird migration, particularly in the books of Job and Jeremiah. Aristotle theorized that birds hibernated, a belief that persisted until as recently as 200 years ago, and others thought birds flew to the moon each winter.

Today, of course, we realize that both of those ideas are incorrect. Still, the only solid conclusions we do have in the hows and whys of migration lead to other unanswered questions. For example, not all birds migrate because of increasingly colder temperatures, as some begin coming south as early as July, when northern conditions are at their optimum, while others don't start until October. In certain species the varying amount of daylight triggers hormonal and metabolic changes but not in others.

And how do birds reach the same destinations year after year? In only a few instances the parents guide their offspring, for in many species the young are the first to leave. Certainly, with their superb vision, birds can and do use specific geographic landmarks to guide them, but many migrate at night as well as in foggy or cloudy weather when such landmarks are not visible.

Some 150 years ago German scientist Alexander von Middendorff hypothesized that birds navigate by an ingrained "magnetic sense" that allows them to determine minute differences in the earth's magnetic field. In other words, birds are born with a compass that tells them which direction to take and when. Surprisingly, such a theory may not be that far off the mark, as more recent studies do seem to show that a small magnet attached to a bird's back can cause it to become severely disoriented, just as the same magnet will cause a mechanical compass to spin.

Today, scientists also wonder what caused birds to begin migrating in the first place. Some say the advancing glacial ice pushed northern birds south, but that does not explain why some species native to nonglaciated areas migrate. Others say birds have been migrating ever since they could fly and that each species reacts differently to environmental changes. In truth, that may be as close to solving the mystery as we'll ever get.

In 1935, scientist F. C. Lincoln published the first formal discussion of migration flyways, the four broad corridors birds generally follow during their north-south movements. Texas receives migrants from the Mississippi and Central flyways (as well as occasional stragglers from the Atlantic and Pacific flyways), which, combined with its warm coastal climate and broad spectrum of habitats, is why it is the best overall winter birding state in the United States.

Some of the amazing migrants that gather in Texas each year are the hummingbirds, and in 1994 during the annual Hummer/Bird Festival in Rockport (see chapter 43), enthusiastic birders voiced the idea of creating a bird observation route along the entire coast. Specific birding hotspots could be pinpointed to take advantage of the sighting opportunities between Beaumont and Brownsville.

The result has been the creation of the Great Texas Coastal Birding Trail, which ultimately will include more than 200 cities along the coast. The purpose of the trail is to promote birding and the spectacular event of migration along the Texas coast, as well as to promote a nature tourism industry throughout the region.

"The Wings of Winter"—Canada geese are common winter residents throughout much of Texas, from the Panhandle to the coast. The birds are particularly abundant in South Texas between Kingsville and Harlingen.

The first phase of the trail, the middle coast, was dedicated at the 1995 Hummer/Bird Festival, with the remainder, the upper and lower coasts, expected to be in place by late 1996.

When completed, winter visitors will find nearly 400 miles of the coast marked with distinctive signs noting the location of each birding site, none more than a half hour's drive from the rest. The work is being sponsored by the Texas Parks and Wildlife Department and the Texas Department of Transportation as well as by local organizations. Although the Great Texas Coastal Birding Trail will provide interesting viewing at all times of the year, it will be particularly exciting during the winter months when the huge population of migrating birds is present. And who knows? Perhaps some keen observer will learn the answer to one of the many questions still unanswered about bird migration.

The Great Texas Coastal Birding Trail (Phase One)

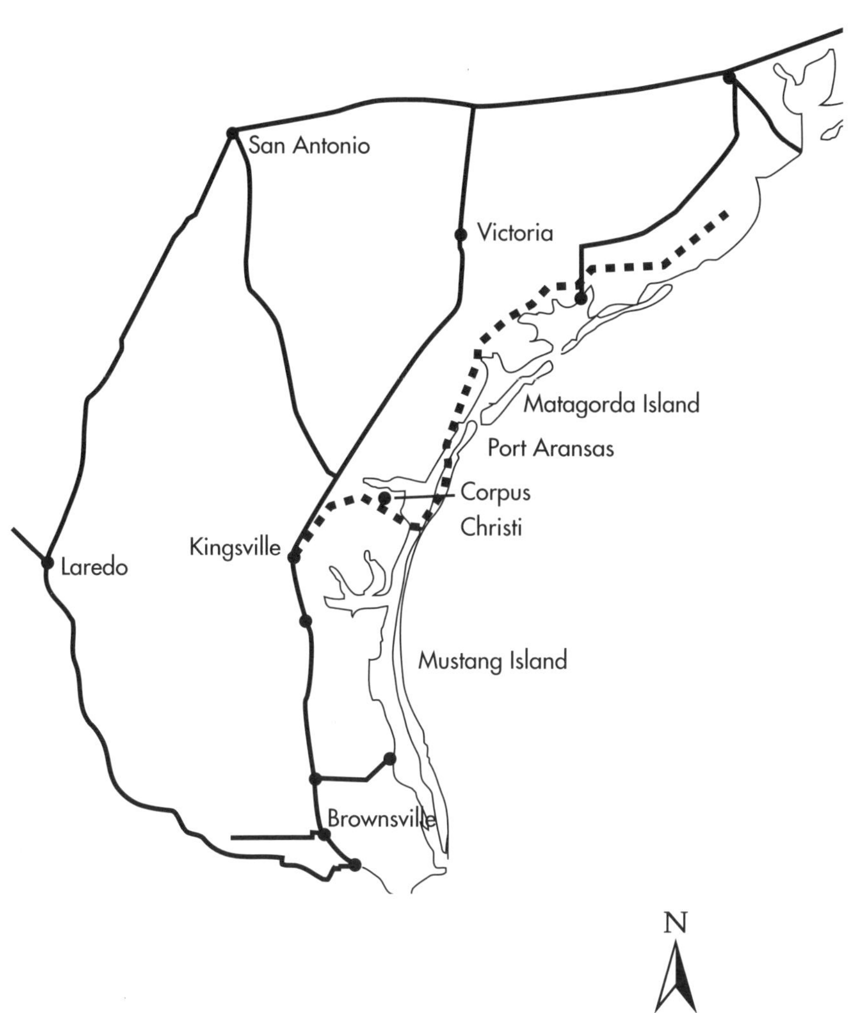

Hot Spots

Phase One of the **Great Texas Coastal Birding Trail**, the Central Texas coast, includes 95 marked sites between Freeport and Baffin Bay on the Laguna Madre (south of the headquarters for Padre Island National Seashore). Included in this area are such well-known spots as the **Welder Wildlife Refuge, Aransas National Wildlife Refuge**, and **Goose Island State Park**, each of which is described elsewhere in this book.

Also included on the trail are many other sites too numerous to list and describe here, but which absolutely deserve any interested birder's attention. More species of birds will be found along this route than in most states. Additional information, maps, and a guidebook (available in 1997) can be obtained by contacting the Nongame Section of the Texas Parks and Wildlife Department or the Rockport-Fulton Area Chamber of Commerce.

2

Wintering Bald Eagles

With the possible exception of the whooping crane, no bird in Texas elicits as much interest as does the bald eagle. Each winter approximately 1,000 of these regal birds migrate into the state, where they spend the months of December, January, and February feeding on the abundant fish found in various lakes and rivers. They are easily viewed, while either perching in the tall pines or gliding high over the water, and in many instances appear to be surprisingly tolerant of human activity. It's almost as if the birds recognize and understand their role in American culture and history.

Adopted as this country's national bird in 1782 by the Continental Congress, the bald eagle has become a worldwide symbol of freedom and democracy. Amazingly, however, these birds were not protected by law in the United States until 1940.

Tens of thousands were shot and poisoned by ranchers who thought eagles attacked and fed on newborn lambs, goats, and calves. Even after Congress passed the Bald Eagle Protection Act in 1940, it took Alaska 20 more years to adopt this law and abolish the bounty it had offered for bald eagles since 1912.

An even greater threat to eagle populations began to appear about 1950. Along Florida's west coast, where eagles had been nesting for centuries, scientists noticed

Today the bald eagle has made a strong recovery from pesticide poisoning, and hundreds winter on freshwater lakes across Texas where they can feed on shad and other fish.

populations beginning to drop. Research eventually pinpointed the reason: Pesticides, most notably DDT, were causing the birds to lay eggs with thin, easily broken shells. In some instances, eggs had no shells at all.

DDT, used heavily in agriculture to control insects, washed into streams and lakes, where it became absorbed by plankton and algae. Small minnows ate the algae and were eaten by larger fish in turn. Thus, the pesticide accumulated in each step of the food chain, with the fish-eating eagles getting the largest dose. By 1967 bald eagle populations had declined so drastically the bird was placed on the Endangered Species List. In 1972 DDT was banned, and in the years since, eagles have made a strong recovery. They have been reclassified to threatened throughout most of their range.

Bald eagles are members of the hawk family and are themselves simply large hawks. There are 50 species of eagles or hawk-eagles in the world, four in North America. Although occasionally seen occupying the same territory, bald eagles are not closely related to the second most popular American eagle, the golden eagle.

Bald eagles, of course, are easily recognized by their white heads and tails. These are found only in mature birds at least four years old. Until the feathers turn white, the birds look somewhat similar to golden eagles, except that they have bright yellow feet and beaks while golden eagles have black bills. Golden eagles also have feathered legs, and bald eagles do not.

Bald eagles mate for life and frequently use the same nest year after year. They build the largest nest of any bird, then add to it each season; an eagle nest in Ohio eventually measured 8 feet across, 12 feet deep, and was estimated to weigh two tons! All this for a clutch of just two eggs annually.

Their primary food is fish, which is why the birds always nest and winter close to water. In addition to plucking live fish off the surface and even stealing an occasional meal from an osprey in flight, eagles are opportunistic scavengers. On Texas lakes they are particularly fond of gizzard shad that are killed by cold water temperatures.

Bald eagles also eat small rodents, particularly those that are injured and present an easy meal. Stories of bald eagles carrying away sheep and goats, however, seem to have little basis in truth, as tests conducted more than half a century ago indicate eagles have difficulty getting off the ground with anything weighing more than just a few pounds.

Hot Spots

One of the most reliable places to view bald eagles is at **Fairfield Lake State Park** near Fairfield, approximately 90 miles south of Dallas. Eagle-watch tours are conducted twice each Saturday, from 10 A.M. to noon and 1 P.M. to 3 P.M., starting in November and continuing through February. The cost is $8 per adult and $4 for children under age 12. In addition, each adult must have a Texas Conservation Passport ($25).

To reach Fairfield Lake State Park, drive south on I-45 from Dallas to Fairfield (Exit 197). In Fairfield turn left on FM 488, follow this 1½ miles, turn right on Park Road 64, and continue on this road 3 miles to the park. Reservations are required and can be made by contacting Fairfield Lake State Park, Rt. 2, Box 912, Fairfield, TX 75840, (903) 389-4514.

Eagle-watch boat tours are also conducted at **Martin Creek Lake State Park** south of Longview. Tours are conducted twice each Saturday and Sunday, 10 A.M. to noon and 2 P.M. to 4 P.M., in December and January. The cost is $8 per adult and $4 for senior citizens and children under age 12.

To reach Martin Creek Lake State Park, exit south on TX Hwy 149 from I-20 in Longview and follow this 18 miles to the city of Tatum. In Tatum turn right on TX Hwy 43 and follow this into the park. Boat accommodations are limited, therefore, advance reservations are recommended. Contact Martin Creek Lake State Park, Rt. 2, Box 20, Tatum, TX 75691, (903) 836-4336.

Still another place to see bald eagles is on the Vanishing Texas River Cruise, conducted every day except Tuesdays from 11 A.M. to 1:30 P.M. on **Lake Buchanan** in Burnet between November and March. Passengers ride in relative comfort aboard a 70-foot, twin-engine, diesel-powered boat with three separate decks. The cost is $15 per adult, $13 for seniors, $10 for children.

To reach the Vanishing Texas dock, drive west from Burnet on TX Hwy 29, turn right (north) on FM 2341 for 14 miles, then turn left at the entrance sign. Advance reservations are needed and can be made by contacting Vanishing Texas River Cruise, Box 901, Burnet, TX 78611, (512) 756-6986.

Boats are not needed to see eagles at **Lake Meredith National Recreation Area** near the city of Borger. The birds can occasionally be spotted during early morning hours near Chimney Hollow Campground on the north end of the lake, especially after prolonged cold weather.

To reach Chimney Hollow, follow FM 1913 south across Big Blue Creek, turn left at the T-intersection as if heading to Blue West Campground. Just before reaching Blue West, look for the sign pointing to Chimney Hollow.

Additional information is available by contacting the Lake Meredith National Recreation Area, P.O. Box 1460, Fritch, TX 79036, (806) 857-3151. There is a bald eagle roost near the lake, but it is located on private property and is not open to the public.

Bald eagles are also present on **Lake Texoma** near Denison, where the birds are frequently seen perched in tall trees along the Texas side of the lake. No organized tours are offered, and a boat is needed to see the birds; they are rarely seen by auto.

The same is true at **Lake o' the Pines** north of Marshall off U.S. Hwy 59, although occasionally birds can be spotted at the overlook by the dam. Drive north on U.S. 59 to Jefferson, exit north on TX Hwy 49, turn left on FM 729, then left again on FM 726, which leads over the dam.

3

Gull Watching

Among all the birds that winter along the Texas coast, the various species of gulls are perhaps the most paradoxical. They're not particularly strong fliers, but many of them migrate thousands of miles annually from their nesting grounds in Alaska and Canada. They are excellent swimmers, but rarely are they seen actually swimming. And while they're famous as scavengers, they're equally famous as robbers. They are also among the few birds that can drink both freshwater and saltwater.

All of which combines to make them fascinating subjects to watch during a winter visit to the coast. Actually, there is no such bird as a "seagull." There are more than 40 different species of gulls around the world, four of which are often found in Texas. These include the herring, the ring-billed, Bonaparte's, and the black-headed laughing gull, which nests along the coast.

The most common of the winter gulls in Texas is the herring gull, easily recognized with its gray wings (with black tips), white underside, and more important, sheer numbers. This is the most widely distributed of the gulls in the United States; its name derives from the fact that it feeds on herring and other small fish forced to the surface by larger predators.

Herring gulls, however, are really nature's original beach patrol, as they also eat the garbage left by tourists. These are the birds you most often see walking along the beachfront or flying over the sidewalks, hovering by the hundreds around shrimp boats in the Gulf, and following the ferry between Galveston and Bolivar Islands. If you want to attract them, all you need to do is take a loaf of bread to the beach and start throwing small pieces into the air. Within minutes you'll be surrounded by dozens of birds.

Laughing gulls are usually part of any gull gathering along the coast. They're smaller than herring gulls and can be distinguished by their black heads and a dark mantle that blends into their black wing tips. They're scavengers, but they've also been observed stealing food from pelicans. After a brown pelican dives and returns to the surface with a pouch full of fish, a laughing gull will occasionally land on the pelican's head and take the fish right out of its bill!

A third species of gull often seen along the winter coast is the ring-billed gull, which, true to its name, has a small dark ring around its bill. Overall, its color closely matches that of the herring gull, but it is smaller in size.

The Bonaparte's is the smallest of the native North American gulls, and can usually be identified by a distinct blackish spot in the white feathers behind each eye, bright red legs, and black bill. It is not as common in Texas as some of the other gulls.

As mentioned previously, gulls aren't particularly strong fliers, even though some, like the ring-billed gull, nest as far north as Alaska and migrate south each winter. They travel on air currents—thermal updrafts—and can soar for hours with hardly a wing beat. In a strong wind, these thermals actually get blown over so they lie horizontally and become a perfect highway for the gulls.

Once the gulls locate a pleasing section of beach, an inland lake, or other area, they tend to return year after year. There are records of individual birds, recognized by distinct markings, visiting the same spot annually for more than 20 years.

Gulls have their place in history, too. In Salt Lake City there is a monument to the California gull, commemorating its arrival in the region to eat hordes of grasshoppers and thus saving the Mormon crops. This species of gull is more common on the plains than on the coast and even today performs a valuable service to farmers and ranchers by eating insects.

Gulls certainly must like the Texas coast, for the birds have been coming each winter for as long as anyone can remember. They're so common they're hardly noticeable, but when watched and studied, they're among the most interesting of the winter birds.

Hot Spots

Gulls are easily viewed along the entire Texas coast in the winter, but one of the more interesting places to view them on the upper Texas coast is **Texas Point National Wildlife Refuge** at Sabine Pass. Follow TX Hwy 87 from Port Arthur approximately 15 miles, and follow it to the right at Sabine Pass. Look for a small entrance sign on the left; it leads into a grass parking lot, and from there you'll have to walk through the marsh to the beach. The best part is you'll likely have the entire beach to yourself in winter.

Gulls are also common along the beach at **Sea Rim State Park,** reached by following Hwy 87 south from Texas Point NWR about 5 miles.

If you take the free ferry from **Port Bolivar** (approximately 30 miles south from Sabine Pass on TX Hwy 87) to Galveston, you'll see plenty of gulls following beside the ferry. Again, they will hardly flap their wings; they're gliding on the obstruction current of air as it deflects upward from the sides of the boat.

In Galveston, look for gulls all along Seawall Boulevard, in the Corpus Christi area, and they are common in Goose Island State Park and the Padre Island National Seashore. To reach **Goose Island State Park,** follow TX Hwy 35 north from Rockport 12 miles, cross the causeway bridge, and turn right on Park Road 13.

To enter the **Padre Island National Seashore,** drive east on Padre Island Drive (TX Hwy 358) to Park Road 22. Continue south for 13 miles to the seashore entrance.

4

Desert Bighorns

In Texas whenever the words "desert bighorn sheep" are mentioned, you might as well be talking about a ghost, for few casual observers have ever seen this most regal of game animals in the wild. That's because it lives where the living is hard—in the ragged, rocky crags, spires, and canyons of some of the state's most rugged mountains. January is a good month for possible bighorn viewing because the weather is cooler and more enjoyable.

There's another reason, as well, which is that there aren't very many of them. In fact, the last native desert bighorn was sighted around 1960. What roams the western ranges today are small scattered bands of animals the Texas Parks and Wildlife Department has been working to re-introduce since 1957.

It has been a long and difficult process, with slow climbs of success followed by sudden drops into failure. Penned animals have reproduced successfully, only to fall prey to mountain lions or disease. Continued efforts to breed and release the bighorns at several different sites, however, have resulted in free-ranging herds totaling about 300 head.

It is doubtful that the desert bighorn was ever as numerous as other game animals, simply by the limiting factors of its habitat. The Spanish explorer Francisco Coronado mentions them in his journal in 1540, and pictographs in caves near El Paso tell the story of prehistoric sheep hunts, but never did bighorn populations approach those of bison or antelope.

In more recent times, bighorn populations were decimated by market hunting. Professional hunters, hired to shoot game to feed railroad and mining camps, preferred sheep because its delicious meat brought the highest prices. As early as the turn of the century, bighorns had been eliminated from much of their historic range. Illegal hunting, the introduction of domestic sheep, and natural predation finished the job.

So why such intensive efforts to re-introduce an animal few today have ever seen? The answer is not only because desert bighorns are part of the historic natural tapestry of Texas, but also because there is a mystique surrounding them unmatched by any other game animal in North America.

Powerful, agile, graceful, and strong are but a few of the adjectives that describe the bighorns. Their physical appearance alone suggests royalty. Mature rams, which weigh up to 300 pounds, are crowned with heavy, spiraling horns that may measure 36 inches around the curve. These horns are never shed and, in fact, produce annual growth rings that tell the animal's age. During the August-to-September breeding season, the horns determine herd dominance, as the rams crash into each other like locomotives until one animal finally concedes.

Today biologists classify the Texas desert bighorn as *Ovis canadensis mexicana,* part of the larger family of bighorns known as *Ovis canadensis canadensis.* Most believe America's wild sheep crossed the land bridge from Asia and that the desert bighorns eventually wandered as far south as northern Mexico, where they adapted to the harsh environment. Other wild sheep remained farther north and eventually evolved into the white Dall sheep of Alaska, the Stone sheep of western Canada, and the Rocky Mountain bighorn of the western United States.

All the bighorns are creatures of wild, remote, but open spaces where their extraordinary vision provides a first line of defense. The terrain itself is their second defense; when threatened, they go up, climbing, jumping, and running easily into impossible places.

Strangely, the desert bighorns probably put more stress on themselves than do their enemies, and in this respect they are quite fragile animals. When they find a place they like, they stay there. Their habitat normally supports only a relatively small number of animals, and when overpopulation occurs, many simply do not survive.

The desert bighorns in Texas today have come from Arizona, Utah, Nevada, and Mexico, and they have been established in five locations in the southwestern part of the state. Additional stockings into new areas are planned in the years ahead.

Hot Spots

The first desert bighorn viewing area for the public is to be completed in late 1996. This will be a 6-mile driving tour at **Elephant Mountain Wildlife Management Area.** The tour will include a small shelter where observers can stop and study the slopes of Elephant Mountain for sheep. Additional tour stops will identify the different types of habitat on this 23,000-acre refuge.

To reach the management area, follow TX Hwy 118 south from Alpine for 26 miles to the entrance. For information, write the Elephant Mountain Wildlife Management Area, Texas Parks and Wildlife Department, HC 65, Box 80, Alpine, TX 79830, (915) 364-2228.

5

January Shorttakes

Green Jays

Among the many January surprises in the brush and mesquite of the Rio Grande Valley is the blue jay that's green. It is a noisy, bold, gregarious, and curious bird like its close cousin, but the green jay is usually considered much prettier. The green jay has green overall plumage with some yellow in its tail feathers, a blue crown, a black throat, and a white band across its forehead. Once seen, it is easily identified and not soon forgotten, for it is a tropical bird living on the edge of some of the harshest country in Texas—the only place in the United States it calls home. Southward, the green jay's range extends to the northernmost regions of South America.

At **Bentsen–Rio Grande Valley State Park** near Mission, drive along Park Road 43, turn left as if going into the picnicking area but then turn right into the RV/trailer campground. Look along both sides of the road for green jays visiting feeders.

6

A Closer Look: Bobwhites and Other Quail

To many bird lovers, seeing, hearing, actually feeling the sudden rise of a covey of quail ranks as one of the supreme experiences of all outdoors. The ground itself erupts, coming alive with a whir of wings and brown bullets hurtling upward and outward through brush and bramble at breakneck speed. It lasts only seconds, then the birds are gone.

Bobwhites are among the most popular game birds in America, and they are common throughout much of Texas, particularly west of a line between Dallas and Houston. The birds are extremely adaptable and survive in fields and pastures, dry grasslands, woods, and even seemingly barren cactus and mesquite flats. January is a good time to see them because they're in coveys rather than alone.

Bobwhites are one of four species of quail native to Texas. The other three are Gambel's, Montezuma, and scaled quail. Each of these is far less numerous and not even that close in overall appearance to the bobwhite, but all are related as members of the broad-based pheasant family. This means the little eight-ounce birds share the family tree not only with pheasants but also with the exotic peacocks. What the four Texas quail do have in common is that they are monogamous for the breeding season; cock and hen share nesting and chick-raising duties; they are not migratory; and they have four-toed, clawed feet adapted for scratching in the ground.

Because the bobwhites are more numerous, they are among the most easily recognized. Overall, the birds are brown to reddish brown in color with short black bills. The male has a conspicuous white stripe above its eyes and a white throat. In spring the males stake out a territory and begin uttering the familiar "bob, bob white!" call. They're trying to attract a hen, and once they do, the marriage is set. Neither bird will mate or stray until after the chicks are raised. The male will even finish incubating a clutch of eggs if the hen is killed.

An average of about 14 eggs is laid in a small but covered depression in the grass. Incubation takes 23 days from the time the final egg is laid, and the chicks weigh less than an ounce when born. Two weeks later they can fly.

Throughout the summer and early fall, the family remains together, feeding, dusting, and watering over a fairly small territory. At night the birds roost in a tight circle on the ground, tails together, heads pointed out.

As autumn approaches, the family groups begin to wander more, eventually meeting and joining other family groups. The resulting coveys, which can number 50 birds or more (most are smaller), remain together throughout the winter. As spring approaches, the males begin to separate to establish their own territories, and the cycle begins anew.

While the bobwhite does not hesitate to take flight in a sudden upward leap, the Montezuma quail sits motionless when alarmed. Named after the famous Aztec chieftain, the Montezuma quail is found in Texas

The bobwhite quail is one of the most popular game birds in Texas and is easily identified by its distinct "bobwhite" call.

only in the rugged Davis Mountains, where it feeds on the grasses, seeds, nuts, and fruits in the oak canyons.

This is one of the most handsome of the quail clan, featuring a bluish beak and a largely white face with a light tan crest extending back over the neck. The body feathers are cinnamon brown, often flecked with white on the breast.

Another crested quail in Texas is the Gambel's, but while the crest of the Montezuma quail follows the curvature of the head down to the neck, the crest of the Gambel's tilts forward like a tiny plume. The bird has brown, black, and white head coloration with a black face, tannish brown body feathers, and reddish brown flanks.

Gambel's quail live in the arid mesquite and willow thickets of far western Texas near El Paso. They are much more numerous in the western and southwestern states and are sometimes known as Arizona quail. They're flight speedsters like the bobwhite, but Gambel's quail roost in trees, and they've adapted to their desert environment by learning to eat cactus.

The fourth quail in Texas is the scaled quail, also known as the blue quail or the "cotton top." It inhabits the grasslands and brush of the Texas Panhandle southward and westward to the lower Rio Grande Valley. Overall, it prefers dry, barren terrain. The names come from the look of the bird's feathers. Its gray body feathers have a definite scale-like appearance, while the head plumage is a distinct white, brushy crest.

While the bobwhite flies and the Montezuma quail sits tight, the scaled quail runs when frightened, although the birds are hesitant to leave a permanent water supply and can become so trustful as to be quite approachable. In winter, large coveys of well over 50 birds are sometimes encountered.

February

Notes

7

Long-billed Curlews

When one thinks of sandpipers, the usual image is of a small, grayish brown bird scampering back and forth along a beach, following each retreating wave as it slides back into the ocean, then outracing the next one that comes crashing in. This description fits several of the 51 members of the sandpiper family, but it does not accurately portray the long-billed curlew. Weighing as much as two pounds, these are not only the largest of the sandpipers but also the largest of all the shorebirds.

Long-billed curlews frequently walk the beaches in the company of their small cousins, but because they are good swimmers, they will just as often feed in the shallows with rafting ducks. Even more frequently, they will be found in open fields where they chase grasshoppers and other insects.

As their name suggests, these birds have an unusually long bill, which may be more than eight inches in length. It curves downward in a graceful arc, in contrast to the upward-curving bills of the godwits which are also members of the sandpiper family. The curve is an evolutionary adaptation that allows the curlews to probe for a wide variety of food including insects, worms, snails, crustaceans, and crabs. They even eat berries.

In Audubon's time, long-billed curlews were seen in huge flocks east of the Mississippi but today the birds are extremely rare there. A close relative, the Eskimo curlew, was nearly hunted to extinction, and some believe the long-billed population is in a steady decline. They have not been studied as thoroughly as some other species, but the observations that have been made provide interesting clues to how the birds live.

The majority of long-billed curlews nest in Alberta and Saskatchewan, laying four eggs in a simple ground nest. There are recorded instances of two females laying eggs in the same nest and sharing duties, and one instance of a long-bill and a close relative, a willet, also sharing a nest.

Incubation time is nearly a month, and the young are able to move about soon after hatching; they leave the nest within a few hours. In time, the birds will grow into their adult brown plumage, have a wingspan of more than 36 inches, and be able to fly at speeds of around 50 mph. Some long-bills actually remain in Texas and Mexico year-round but most only winter along the coast. Others winter along the southern California coast and through Baja Mexico.

With their long bills and long legs, curlews just seem to belong on a beach. That's what makes it so interesting to see a small flock of them happily maneuvering back and forth in a plowed field miles from the ocean, even occasionally in the grassy parks of coastal cities. They dart here, then there, snatching bugs and caterpillars at each stop. An observer will discover that while the curlews have taken no apparent notice of him, they have quickly moved away. When finally frightened into flight, they do so suddenly and together, as if by prearranged signal. The cry they shriek as they fly to a distant shore or to another field is a distinct "cur-lew!" which gives them their name.

Hot Spots

Long-billed curlews might be seen anywhere along the lower Texas coast between Port O'Connor and Brownsville, but several places seem to attract them more than others.

At **Aransas National Wildlife Refuge,** take the boardwalk by the observation tower to the edge of the beach and scan the shoreline and the shallow water carefully; these are favorite haunts of the long-billed curlew because of the sand, shallow water, and abundant food.

Another good spot is along TX 35 in Rockport. Simply follow the highway south until you see a large bay on your left. This is **Little Bay** and the **Connie Hagar Wildlife Sanctuary.** There is plenty of room to pull over for bird observation here. Look for long-billed curlews in the shallow water and occasionally even on the grass along the water's edge.

Long-billed curlews are also common in **Laguna Atascosa National Wildlife Refuge.** Take the longer Bayside Tour Loop first because it's usually more productive than the much shorter Lakeside Drive. Long-billed curlews are frequently seen along the next 4 miles of beach (the shore of the Laguna Madre) all the way down to Redhead Ridge Overlook. Once the tour road turns away from the water, begin looking for long-billed curlews along the left side of the road anywhere the vegetation is thin and the birds can move freely to chase insects.

8

Winter Bluebirds

Each winter as Texas gradually turns various shades of brown and gray, occasional flashes of blue will suddenly liven the landscape. These are bluebirds, and while some are present throughout the year, February is one of the best months to see them in large numbers; flocks of as many as 20 are occasionally reported in different areas.

In the winter, too, Texas can boast of having all three species of bluebirds, the eastern, mountain, and western, and in some places it is possible to see all three together.

Bluebirds are members of the thrush family, which includes robins as well as blackbirds, and are found at various times of the year from Canada to Mexico. The eastern bluebird is the most well known of the three species, but all three are dearly loved because of their brilliant colors, cheerful songs, and the fact they often live in and near suburban neighborhoods.

The three species are quite similar in that they are primarily blue in color and in each the male is the most colorful. The eastern bluebird has perhaps the brightest blue and is distinguished by its rust-colored breast; the mountain bluebird is more of a turquoise blue; and the western bluebird is similar to the eastern except that its back is also rust.

The bluebird's primary diet consists of insects including grasshoppers, beetles, spiders, bees, and crickets. In the winter months when insects are scarce, the birds rely on various berries.

The eastern bluebird, which lives in Texas all year, appears to be making a strong comeback from near extinction. Less than 50 years ago this bird was common throughout the nation, but in the years following World War II, a combination of habitat loss, severe winters, and growing competition for nesting sites by other birds led to a major decline in the population. Some estimate that as much as 90 percent of the eastern bluebird population was lost in just a few years.

As with nearly all wildlife on the brink of extinction today, habitat loss caused most of the decline. The eastern bluebird was more severely impacted than either the mountain or the western species because its favorite nesting areas are in older trees where hollow cavities have formed, along with rotting stumps and fence posts where similar holes are present. The trees and woodlands used by bluebirds were bulldozed and the wood posts replaced with steel ones.

Concerned citizens across America have largely been responsible for the eastern bluebird's return through the building of bird boxes for nesting and the establishment of trails of these boxes, commonly known as bluebird trails. Bluebird nesting boxes are not new; they've been used for well over a century, as Thoreau describes putting them up himself in his diaries.

Bluebird nesting can begin as early as this month in parts of Texas, with each of the three species laying between three and possibly eight pale blue eggs. Incubation takes two weeks, and less than three weeks later the young are flying.

As soon as the parents get the first brood out of the nest, they begin preparing for a second, and their fledgling brothers and sisters may actually help take care of them, as the young require feeding about once every half hour. In some instances a third brood is raised in late summer.

Hot Spots

Davis Mountains State Park near Fort Davis offers perhaps the best opportunity to see all three species of bluebirds in one location this month. To reach the park, follow TX Hwy 17 north for 1 mile out of Fort Davis, then turn west on TX Hwy 118 for 3 miles to the park entrance on the left. Look for bluebirds along the main drive, Park Road 3, and especially in the full-service campground adjacent to the road. You may also want to sit in the bird-watching blind located behind the park's Interpretive Center (near the campground) and watch for bluebirds in the nearby trees.

Flocks of eastern bluebirds are often observed around the boat ramp and campground at **Martin Dies Jr. State Park,** 12 miles west of Jasper on U.S. Hwy 190. Don't turn into the first entrance into the park on the left, but instead continue on U.S. 190 another mile and turn right into the Walnut Ridge Unit on Park Road 48. Follow this road into the campground and boat launching area and look for bluebirds among the scattered hardwoods.

One of the best-known contacts for up-to-date bluebird information in this part of Texas is Mrs. Mary Reed, who is often described as the Bird Lady of Wildwood because of her work in establishing and monitoring local bluebird trails. She can be reached at Box 816, Village Mills, TX 77663, (409) 834-6239.

Another place to see eastern bluebirds is in the small city of **Wills Point,** located about 50 miles east of Dallas on U.S. Hwy 80. Wills Point has been designated the Bluebird Capital of Texas, and each April the city has a Bluebird Festival, which includes a parade, exhibit, and bus tours of different bluebird trails constructed by area residents. The Wills Point Chamber of Commerce will send a complete schedule of events if you write or telephone them at Box 217, Wills Point, TX 75169, (903) 873-3111.

9

Big Bass on the Move

It has often been said that bass fishing in the South is more than a sport; it is a way of life. In few places is this more evident than in Texas in early spring, when anglers from throughout the state—and many from out of state, as well—converge on the various impoundments to test their skill.

Their quarry is the largemouth bass, *Micropterus salmoides,* described by Dr. James A. Henshall in his classic 1881 *Book of the Black Bass* as "inch for inch, and pound for pound, the gamest fish that swims." For many years, the Texas Parks and Wildlife Department has followed an active stocking and management program for these fish, and as a result, Texas now offers some of the finest fishing in the United States for largemouth bass.

Late winter and early spring are the favorite times to pursue bass because the fish are not only the heaviest they will be all year but also the most accessible. The females are heavy with eggs and are moving into the shallow water to spawn.

Although the exact calendar schedule varies from lake to lake across the state, the general movement of fish into shallow water can begin as early as December and continues in various phases into April. Not all the bass in a lake move shallow at the same moment, and factors such as water temperature can delay or speed up the timetable. Throughout much of Texas, the movement peaks in February and March.

The smaller male bass move shallow first. Their task is to construct a nest suitable for the female to use when depositing her eggs. The male does this by fanning the bottom with his tail, creating a dish or saucer-shaped depression that usually ranges from 12 to about 24 inches in diameter. Bass prefer a fairly hard gravel or sand bottom for the nests; mud or silt bottoms are rarely used.

The depth of these beds can be as shallow as two to three feet or as deep as 10 to 15 feet, and in some lakes the nest is actually made in flooded timber, in the forks and branches of huge trees. Nest building can take as long as two days.

While the male is busy becoming a housekeeper, the larger females remain nearby in slightly deeper water, as if waiting for the exact moment their biological clock tells them to move forward. For some reason not totally understood by biologists, the bass will station themselves right beside trees or bushes, along the edges of channels dropping into deeper water, or over long, sloping points that also extend into deeper depths. This "object and structure orientation" characterizes bass throughout their lives, which is why anglers try to aim their casts to such places.

When the females do move shallow, they do not have a pre-arranged mate. The selection process seems to be most of the male's doing, as he physically guides a female to his nest. Depending on her size, she may be carrying as many as 150,000 eggs, which she quickly releases into the nest. The male, stationing himself beside her, releases his milt at the same time; the entire process takes only a few minutes.

Largemouth bass have been following this same cycle of reproduction for perhaps 50 million years. They are native to North America and were totally unknown to the earliest European explorers who reached these shores. Various tribes of southern Native Americans knew the largemouth, however, including the Seminoles, who fished for them with lures made of deer hair, according to observations made in the 1760s by naturalist William Bartram.

Today the largemouth can be found in every state except Alaska, and in many countries in Europe, Africa, and South America. The reasons for its tremendous popularity are perfectly illustrated by conditions in Texas: The fish are found in lakes, ponds, streams, and rivers everywhere; and they grow to enormous size.

In 1932 Georgia angler George Perry caught the fish that is currently classified as holding the world record for largemouth bass: 22 pounds, 4 ounces. Only Texas and California have come close to the record, California with several fish over the 20-pound mark, and Texas with several over 17 pounds.

With their thousands of eggs in the springtime, female bass can be as much as two to three pounds heavier before spawning than afterward, which is why anglers pursue them so ardently this time of year. Although some of these big bass are kept as wall-mounted trophies by the anglers who catch them, many are donated to the Texas Parks and Wildlife Department.

In the department's State Fish Hatchery in Tyler, technicians attempt to get the fish to spawn under controlled conditions, after which they are tagged and eventually released into the lake from which they were caught. This program, which started in 1986, is known

Some of the heaviest largemouth bass of the year are caught in February and March when they begin moving into shallow water. Nearly all, including this twelve pounder, are released safely.

as Operation Share A Lunker, and only fish 13 pounds and heavier are accepted. The program has gained national attention from other state agencies because of its phenomenal success. Several of the tagged trophy bass have actually been caught—and released—a second time.

Hot Spots

Lake Fork has produced 37 of the top 50 heaviest bass in the state, including the state record 18.18-pound bass caught in January 1992. The impoundment is located approximately 75 miles east of Dallas near the towns of Quitman, Alba, and Emory. To reach the lake, follow I-20 east from Dallas, turn north on U.S. 69 at Lindale, then east on Farm Road 515 in Emory. Marinas, which include motels, restaurants, and guide services, are numerous around the lake.

Another hotspot is **Sam Rayburn Reservoir,** a larger impoundment east of Lufkin. Although Rayburn has not produced any 17-pound bass, anglers regularly catch 10- to 12-pound bass here in the spring. Key cities around the lake are Lufkin, Jasper, and San Augustine.

Lufkin is located at the junction of U.S. Highways 69 and 59; following 69 south from Lufkin 22 miles to Zavalla and turning left on TX Hwy 63 will take you to Jasper. San Augustine can be reached by following U.S. 96 north from Jasper approximately 50 miles. By taking TX 147 northeast from Zavalla, you can cross the lake and also reach San Augustine.

Another popular reservoir is **Lake Falcon,** located in South Texas at the city of Zapata. Follow I-35 southwest from San Antonio to Laredo, then turn left (south) onto U.S. 83 just before the international bridge and follow it 50 miles to Zapata. Again, numerous motels, restaurants, and fishing guide services are available.

Valid Texas state fishing licenses are required

for any angler over the age of 16; they are available at tackle shops, marinas, and even some motels near the lakes.

Additional information on these and other Texas lakes is available from the Texas Parks and Wildlife Department, 4200 Smith School Road, Austin, TX 78744, (512) 389-4800.

10

Contemplating Dinosaurs

It seems hard to believe now that at one time most of Texas was under water and even harder to believe that when it was, dinosaurs roamed across much of the state. A hundred million years ago the Gulf of Mexico lapped over what is now the Dallas–Fort Worth metroplex. It covered the future Big Bend National Park to the southwest and even what would become Guadalupe Mountains National Park to the west.

The water was shallow, and the region was more a series of mud flats, swamps, and lagoons where leafy vegetation grew abundantly. The climate was warm, as it is today, but certainly much more humid and subtropical. In short, it was perfect habitat for a variety of dinosaurs, the huge but rather placid plant eaters as well as the more violent carnivores that fed on them.

Dinosaurs lived on the earth for more than 140 million years, and indications are that they walked across Texas during most of that time. Of the dozens of different species that evolved, 16 have been identified in the state. Tracks and skeletal remains have been located in more than 20 counties, ranging from Grayson and Montague counties along the Oklahoma state line to far west Hudspeth County near the Mexican border.

One of the oldest fossils in the state has been identified as technosaurus, a four-foot plant eater that walked on its hind legs. It was named after Texas Tech University because the first remains were unearthed nearby. Coelophysis, an eight-foot, 100-pound meat eater that probably fed often on technosaurus, is another dinosaur whose fossilized bones have been found in Texas. It was a fast runner with a voracious appetite; some scientists believe it may have even cannibalized its own young. Other dinosaurs that ruled Texas include tyrannosaurus, the fearsome seven-ton meat eater with jaws three feet deep, and pleurocoelus, a 50-foot plant eater that weighed about 45 tons—a brontosaurus-type creature.

Although Texas is seldom thought of as a center for dinosaur study—fossil finds are much more numerous in states farther west—what has been found here has shed fascinating insight on how these huge reptiles lived. For example, a cluster of large tracks surrounding smaller tracks found in Bandera County was among the first to indicate dinosaurs had a social structure and traveled in herds, with adults forming a protective circle around their young. Other tracks prove dinosaurs could walk without having to drag their tails for balance. February is a good time for dinosaur study because of the generally agreeable weather that permits outdoor activities like this.

At Dinosaur Valley State Park, tracks reveal an even more intriguing tale. Along the bed of the Paluxy River are the tracks of a 40-foot pleurocoelus. Beside them are the tracks of a smaller but vicious enemy, the two-footed, carnivorous acrocanthosaurus, which weighed about three tons. Pleurocoelus was a fairly sociable dinosaur because it generally lived in herds, but apparently it was caught in the open by itself. The last tracks show where the attack began.

The end of the dinosaurs came about 65 million years ago, but scientists can only theorize as to what caused their extinction. Ideas range from a sudden natural disaster that cooled the earth's temperature and caused plant life to die, to a gradual series of geologic and climatic changes to which the dinosaurs could not adjust. For 140 million years, however, the giant reptiles and thunder lizards roamed Texas, and we are all richer because they did.

Unfortunately, the majority of dinosaur fossils and tracks have been found on private property that is not open to the public. Even excavations now in progress are closed to all but qualified paleontologists.

The most dramatic place to see evidence of Texas dinosaurs is in **Dinosaur Valley State Park,** located just south of the city of Glen Rose in Somervell County. Tracks here were first discovered in 1909 and rate as some of the finest in the world; a set excavated in 1938 is on display in the American Museum of Natural History in New York.

To reach the park, drive south through Glen Rose on U.S. Highway 67. Just before crossing the Paluxy River, turn right on County Road 205 and follow it 4 miles to Park Road 59. Turn right, and follow 59 one mile to the park entrance.

Once in the Dinosaur Valley, take time to see the exhibit and the videotape program in the Visitor's Center before going out to view the tracks. You'll have a much clearer understanding of what you'll be seeing.

From the Visitor's Center, signs point the way to the tracks, which are located both in the bed of the Paluxy River and along one shore. Rocks have been strategically placed in the water so you can cross to see where the dramatic pleurocoelus and acrocanthosaurus fight took place.

For additional information, contact the Park Superintendent, Dinosaur Valley State Park, Box 396, Glen Rose, TX 76043, (817) 897-4588.

Less than a mile beyond the park entrance on County Road 205, visitors can also view about 50 tracks on **the property of Jacob McFall.** While tracks in the state park are frequently under water during times of heavy rain, the McFall tracks are on higher ground and can still be seen. Signs on the road indicate the entrance to the property. The fee is $4 per automobile.

Fossilized remains of different dinosaurs excavated in Texas can only be seen in museums. Among the facilities open to the public are the Strecker Museum at Baylor University (Fourth and State, Waco 76798, 871-755-1110); Texas Tech Museum (Fourth and Indiana, Lubbock 79409, 806-742-2442); Panhandle Plains Museum (2401 4th Avenue, Canyon 79015, 806-656-2244); Witte Museum (3801 Broadway, San Antonio 78209, 210-820-2111); Museum of Science and History (1500 Montgomery Street, Fort Worth 76107, 871-732-1631); Museum of Natural History (3535 Grand, Dallas 75226, 214-431-3466); Museum of Science (One Harmon Circle Drive, Houston 77030, 713-639-4629); and the Natural History Museum (1090 North Chaparral, Corpus Christi 78401, 512-883-2862).

Nutria in Anahuac National Wildlife Refuge

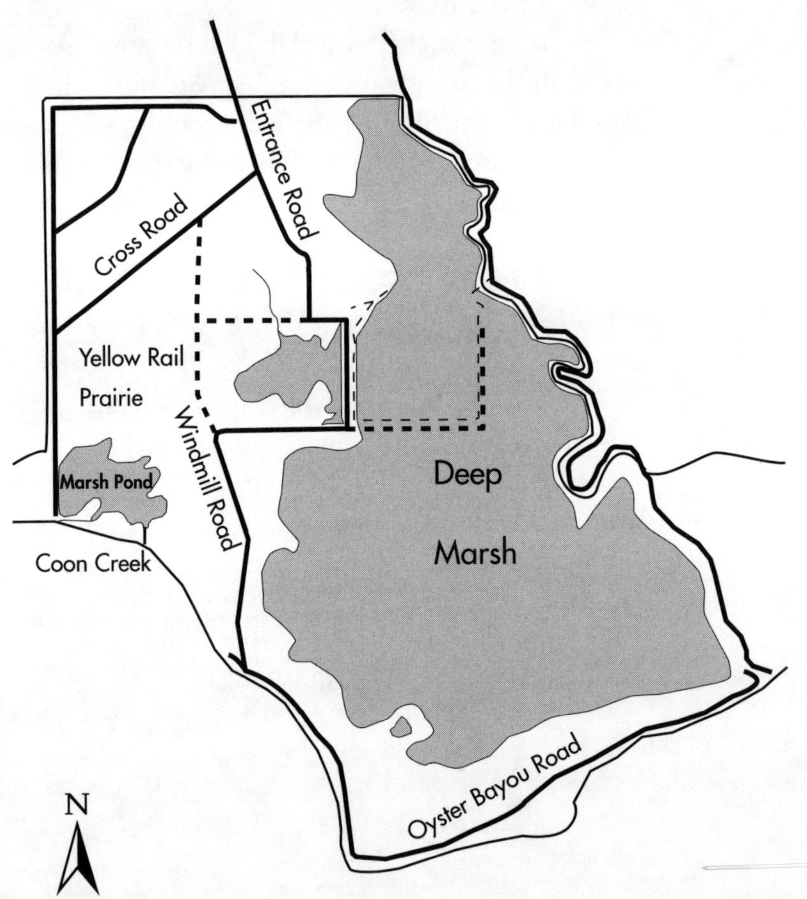

11

February Shorttakes

Nesting Nutria

The nutria *(Myocastor coypus)* is a prime example of a money-making scheme gone astray. Nutria are large rodents, slightly heavier than muskrats but smaller than beavers. They are native to South America but were brought into the United States earlier this century to become a possible source of fur. Some eventually escaped from fur ranches, and others were actually released to help control vegetation.

They have spread into a number of areas of the Southeast, where, in some cases, they have replaced the native muskrats. It's easy to see how after a visit this month to **Anahuac National Wildlife Refuge**, where nutria nest on small mounds of vegetation throughout the marsh. The young will be out, and it's possible to see dozens of them along any of the auto tour roads. Unlike beaver or muskrat, these interesting mammals are not easily frightened by humans and generally remain in plain view.

For directions to Anahuac National Wildlife Refuge, see chapter 69.

The collared peccary, or javelina, is a common sight throughout much of South and West Texas. The animals often travel in huge groups that may number several dozen animals.

12

A Closer Look: The Javelina

Over the course of time, a number of mammals have migrated northward from their original home in South America up through Central America and Mexico and eventually into Texas. One of these, seen frequently this month in the thorny brush country of South and West Texas, is the javelina, or collared peccary.

Despite its coarse black and gray hair and short, stubby appearance, the javelina is not a member of the pig family. It is part of the peccary family and has no relatives in the United States. The name "collared" comes from the narrow ring of lighter hair around its neck.

Rumors concerning the fierceness of javelina abound, but in truth the animal is rarely aggressive to human beings unless cornered or defending its young. Its eyesight is among the poorest of all game animals and its hearing is only moderately good. Its keenest sense by far is that of smell.

Should a fight begin, however, javelina are well equipped to do considerable damage by way of their four canine teeth, which are not visible unless the animal opens its mouth. These teeth are positioned in the mouth so that the uppers and lowers rub against each other constantly, keeping them not only fairly short but also extremely sharp. Javelina do not have tusks, as many have been led to believe.

When fights occur, other javelina often join the fray. This is probably because the herds in which they travel are actually family groups that may number as many as 25 to 30 individuals. They have a fairly well-defined home range or territory, which is normally several hundred acres.

Feeding across this home range takes up most of their daylight hours, especially in colder weather. Prickly pear cactus, mesquite beans, and berries make up their primary diet, but javelina probably eat most types of vegetation found in their range. In times of drought, the prickly pear also provides fluid.

In parts of western Texas, ranchers often feed cottonseed to the whitetail deer on their ranges, and when available this is also a favorite food for javelina. Under cover of darkness, a herd of the little marauders will march right into a yard or feedlot where the cottonseed is stored and begin gorging themselves. Some animals eat so much they fall asleep where they stand—the same thing that happens when barnyard pigs discover corn.

The young can be born any time of year, although small litters (often only one individual) are born most often in spring and early fall. The young javelina are more brown than black; the dark black and gray coloration doesn't appear for several months.

In the early part of this century javelina were often hunted for their hides and because they were thought to compete with cattle for grass. In Texas, the animals were finally granted game-animal status in the 1970s, and today they are protected by law with an established hunting season and bag limit.

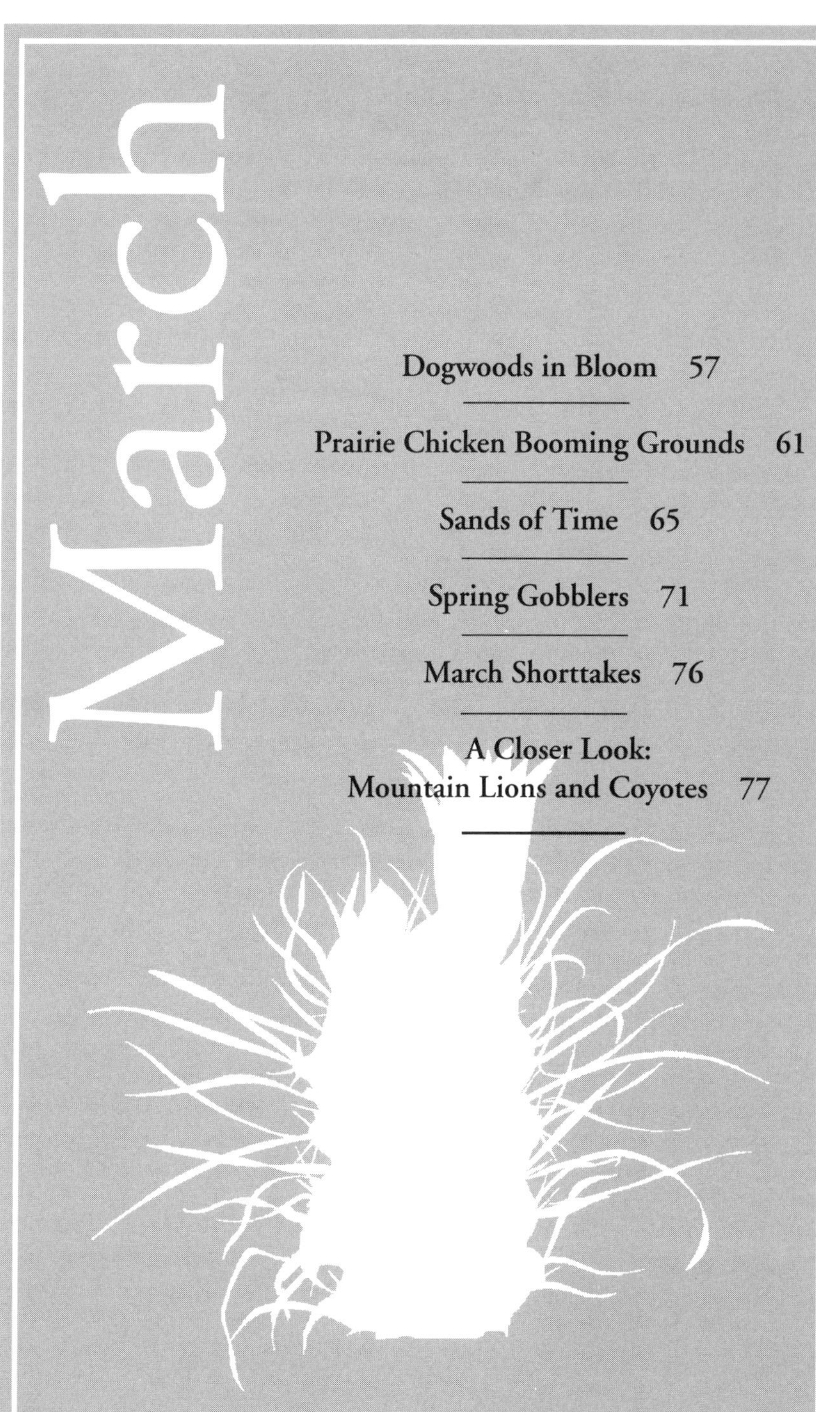

March

Notes

13

Dogwoods in Bloom

Each March, the normally green forests of East Texas turn white and pink as one of America's favorite trees, the flowering dogwood, blooms. These small, colorful trees thrive only in the rich, moist conditions of the Pineywoods and the eastern third of the state; they are seldom found in the drier regions to the west.

There are more than 100 different species of dogwood around the world, with approximately 40 of them found in North America. Only seven of these, however, actually reach tree size. The rest are shrubs. Various dogwoods have been cultivated for more than 250 years, and today they continue to be popular ornamental trees because of their blossoms.

Legend has it that the name *dogwood* derives from the fact that in old England the bark of this tree was often mixed with water to produce a tonic used to wash mangy dogs. There may be some truth to this, as the bark certainly does have medicinal qualities. Dried dogwood bark ground into powder and boiled in water to produce a tea was used by the Confederacy to treat malaria when cinchona bark, the source of quinine, was not available. Drinking the tea produces a sweat and helps break fever, a remedy that was in use until relatively modern times.

Another legend that perhaps has even more basis in truth is that *dogwood* may be a derivation of the word *daggerwood,* which refers to the past practice of cutting this wood into thin sticks to skewer meats and vegetables for grilling. The reason this theory is plausible is because the genus name for dogwood is the Latin word *Cornus,* which many translate as meaning "tough wood." It has also led to the name "cornel wood." Over the years, dogwood has been used in the manufacture of a variety of articles, including wheel hubs, tool handles, barrel hoops, and even engraver's blocks, all of which require extreme hardness.

Book Five of the epic poem *Aeneid,* in which Virgil describes the Greek war against Troy, mentions soldiers carrying lances made of what may have been dogwood: "They wear on their hair ceremonial garlands, well trimmed, / And each of them carries a couple of steel-tipped cornel-wood lances."

In Texas, the flowering dogwood is the most common of the dogwoods, but others include the roughleaf dogwood, the silky dogwood, and the stiff cornel dogwood. In all, the wood is whitish and tight grained, but none of the trees grow large enough to have any commercial value.

The bright red berries of dogwood, which appear in September and October, are a valuable food source for many different species of wildlife including birds, deer, and squirrels. The berries are poisonous to humans, however.

Originally, both the water tupelo and the black tupelo, which are also found in East Texas, were considered members of the dogwood family, but botanists have since decided there are enough differences for those trees to be classified in their own family.

Hot Spots

Some of the best places to see flowering dogwoods this month are in the **Angelina National Forest** near Zavalla. Practically any of the various county roads branching off TX Hwy 63 south out of Zavalla will pass through dogwoods. Among the best are the roads leading to Boykin Springs, Caney Creek, and the Plum Ridge and Sandy Creek recreation areas.

Dogwoods can also be seen by following TX Hwy 147 north from Zavalla across Sam Rayburn Reservoir to Broaddus, then taking FM 83 east toward Pineland. Along this route the roads leading to Harvey Creek Park, Coleman Cover, and Rayburn Park also offer good views of flowering dogwoods.

From Pineland, follow FM 83 north to Hemphill, then turn south on TX Hwy 87 for 5 miles to the junction of FM 2426. This will take you back to Pineland (10 miles) and give you a quick but pleasant tour in the **Sabine National Forest.** As in the Angelina, practically any of the U.S. Forest Service roads here will provide excellent dogwood viewing.

Another favorite dogwood viewing area is the **Davy Crockett National Forest** east of Crockett. Take TX Hwy 7 east from Crockett to Ratcliff, then follow FM 227 north 7 miles to the junction with TX Hwy 21. If you turn left on 21, this will lead you back to Crockett. You'll see dogwoods all along the route.

The cities of Palestine and Woodville also have dogwood festivals. For dates and maps, contact the Palestine Chamber of Commerce at (800) 659-3484 or the Woodville Chamber of Commerce at (409) 283-2632.

The Attwater's prairie chicken has become one of America's most endangered species due to loss of habitat. Less than a hundred remain in the wild at the Attwater National Wildlife Refuge; a captive-breeding program has been initiated at the Fossil Rim Wildlife Center near Glen Rose.

14

Prairie Chicken Booming Grounds

The ritual normally begins just after daybreak on March mornings when a small, brownish, chickenlike bird slips out of the tall prairie grasses and moves into a clearing. It puffs out its throat to produce two highly visible yellow-orange sacs, raises a bonnet of short head feathers, and begins stamping its tiny feet as if running in place.

At the same time, the bird begins producing a low, deep "ooo-ooo-looo" call. This is known as "booming," and it is the mating ballet of the Attwater's prairie chicken, a member of the grouse family today found only in Texas. It is quite possibly one of the most endangered species in the world; in late 1995 the total wild population was estimated to be 68 birds.

The Attwater's *(Tympanuchus cupido attwateri)* is named after University of Texas professor and conservationist Henry P. Attwater, who wanted to distinguish it from its close relatives, the greater and lesser prairie chickens. In the past, the Attwater's range extended over six to eight million acres across both the Texas and Louisiana coastal prairies from Corpus Christi to the Mississippi River, but today the bird survives on less than 200,000 total acres in just six Texas counties. It became extinct in Louisiana in 1919.

The Attwater's belongs to one of about 10 families of birds known as arena birds, which means they perform their courtship displays in very specific places. For the prairie chicken, these areas are known as booming grounds, and the mating ritual is a fascinating spectacle to watch.

The male expands his two air sacs, or tympani, as if inflating balloons. In contrast to other members of the grouse family that produce a rolling drumbeat sound by rapidly flapping their wings, the Attwater's booming comes from these inflated air sacs, and instead of flapping its wings, it stamps its feet in place.

Females are attracted by the strength of both the visual display and the booming. Mating takes place on the booming ground, and nests are made only a short distance away. After mating, however, the male takes no part in nest building, incubating eggs, or raising young. The eggs hatch in approximately 24 days, and within hours the young are out and about feeding; within a week most are flying. The diet includes insects, fruits, leaves, seeds, and grains, depending on the season.

The Attwater's demise has been a rapid one due primarily to loss of habitat. In 1900 the population probably numbered a million birds, but by 1937 the number had dropped to just 8,700. Thirty years later, in 1967, the population had dropped to just over 1,000, but during the next 12 years it climbed again to just over 2,200. Since then, however, the Attwater's has been on a steady decline. By 1993 the population had fallen to an estimated 456 birds, and by 1995 it had dropped even further, to just 68 total birds.

The creation in 1972 of the 8,000-acre Attwater Prairie Chicken National Wildlife Refuge in Colorado County, approximately 50 miles west of Houston, undoubtedly slowed the prairie chicken's slide into history, and two other ongoing programs should add further help. One of these is the captive-breeding program started in 1992 at the Fossil Rim Wildlife Center near Glen Rose (in cooperation with Texas A&M University), and the other is the Galveston Bay Coastal Reserve near Galveston.

In 1992, with assistance from the U.S. Fish and Wildlife Service, Fossil Rim biologists collected 49 wild Attwater's prairie chicken eggs and hatched 45 of them in the Center's incubators. Eventually, some of those birds were bred with others raised from captive laid eggs in 1993.

This successful captive-breeding program led to the re-introduction in August 1995 of 13 male Attwater's prairie chickens to the wild at the refuge. This first release was primarily to test how the birds would survive; a hundred or more might be released in 1996.

At the same time biologists were studying the release of pen-raised birds, Mobil Oil Company donated 2,263 acres of Gulf coast prairie along Galveston Bay to the Nature Conservancy, along with $100,000, for prairie chicken habitat restoration. This tract has since become the Galveston Bay Coastal Reserve, and it presently has a small resident population of 16 Attwater's prairie chickens. It is not open to the public.

Only time will tell if this historic little bird will survive into the 21st century, or follow its ancestor, the heath hen, into extinction. If the Attwater's does survive, it will be a major victory for a dedicated group of conservationists and biologists. If it doesn't and the booming grounds become silent, it will be a major loss for Americans everywhere.

Hot Spots

Fossil Rim Wildlife Center is undoubtedly the most reliable place to see the Attwater's prairie chicken, even though the birds are in large holding pens rather than roaming free. The pens are located in a portion of the center known as the Intensive Management Area, which is open to the public on a limited basis when guided tours are given.

To reach Fossil Rim, drive south on U.S. Highway 67 from Glen Rose approximately 3 miles. Look for signs pointing to the left, where you'll turn and drive another 2 miles to the entrance. For entrance fee and scheduling information, contact the center at Rt. 1, Box 210, Glen Rose, TX 76043, (817) 897-2960.

Due to the low population of wild prairie chickens at the **Attwater Prairie Chicken National Wildlife Refuge,** the chances of actually seeing one there are remote. The known booming ground areas have been closed to the public, although this will definitely change if the pen-raised birds survive and the population expands.

At any rate, a drive or walk through any other portion of the refuge will certainly show you the habitat the birds use, and you'll see other species of wildlife such as sandhill cranes, snow geese and re-introduced native bison.

To reach the refuge, follow TX Hwy 36 from Sealy and turn west on FM 3013. Follow this for 10 miles to the refuge entrance. The refuge is open every day from sunrise to sunset; personnel are on duty from 7:30 A.M. to 4 P.M., Monday through Friday. The address is P.O. Box 519, Eagle Lake, TX 77434, (409) 234-3021.

15

Sands of Time

According to geologists, Texas is around a billion years old and this month, between visits to the dogwood trails and listening to wild turkeys gobble, it may be enjoyable to spend a little time studying Texas's geologic history. There are a lot of places to visit, because Texas was an active region. During the era known as the Precambrian, when much of the earth's geologic history began, Texas had its start as sediment from one of several oceans that covered most of the planet.

Sediments eventually formed huge land masses that became continents, but in the beginning, these continents were not firmly established in place. They moved around in the oceans. Occasionally, one of these continents crashed into another one, and when this happened, the heat buildup from the friction actually turned some of the sediments into molten rock. These rocks piled on top of each other to form mountains and ridges, but then they eroded back down to flatlands as water covered them again. Shallow seas were filled with tiny living organisms like clams and snails, and as these died and settled to the bottom, their shells eventually formed limestone, one of the most dominant rocks in Texas today.

Limestone, as well as other types of rocklike sandstone and shale, continued to be deposited in different

The Lighthouse is perhaps the most well-known rock formation of Palo Duro Canyon State Park and can be reached by a five-mile hiking trail.

layers for the next 150 million years. Shallow seas still covered much of West Texas, but in other regions the water had receded and the first primitive plants began to appear.

After the plants, which gradually evolved from ferns into actual trees about 400 million years ago, came the fish. At the same time, the tremendous pressures created by the continued deposit of various sediments created uplifting and folding. In essence, these were times of awesome earthquakes, the power of which we can only vaguely imagine.

Sometime about 100 million years later, another continental crash occurred, and this one had a profound effect on what would eventually become the final geographical map of Texas. When the continents collided, the Quachita Mountains of eastern Oklahoma and western Arkansas formed, extending southward across Texas from what is now Dallas down to Austin and over to Del Rio. What later would become the

Gulf of Mexico spread up the eastern side of these mountains, while on the western side the land formed a series of deep basins.

Gradually, over more millions of years, this mountain range was eroded and then buried under thousands of feet of sediment as Texas was submerged again, this time under a Gulf of Mexico that spread all the way to the Arctic Ocean. Only around the city of Marathon and in a few areas west of Austin can any remains of the original Ouachitas still be found in Texas.

Sediments from this huge inland sea also formed what became the Guadalupe Mountains in Western Texas around 280 million years ago. These mountains, including the 8,747-foot peak of El Capitan, are actually the exposed end of an ancient reef that continues into New Mexico, then goes underground for about 300 miles in a long loop and surfaces again near Alpine, Texas.

Other ancient rock formations are also visible throughout parts of western Texas. Whenever you see very reddish sandstone, you're looking at something 250 million years old—rocks older than the dinosaurs.

The dinosaurs came and went. The Rocky Mountains uplifted, not only sending their own rolling blanket of rocky debris across much of Texas but also creating rivers that began carrying even more sediment to the Gulf, actually pushing the shoreline farther and farther south. That's why East Texas today provides some of the most organically rich land in the state.

In the west, the heaving and buckling of the Rockies caused other lesser ranges to form, such as the Franklin Mountains near El Paso. Volcanoes began erupting southwest of Austin, and later massive eruptions occurred near what is now Big Bend National Park.

The last major uplift occurred 10 million years ago and created what is known today as the Edwards Plateau across Central Texas. It also elevated the Panhandle of North Texas. As a result, the rivers from the Rockies carrying sediment to East Texas and the Gulf were forced to begin carving their way through new ground, creating Palo Duro and Caprock Canyons.

Hot Spots

Palo Duro Canyon offers the chance to see the last 250 million years of geologic history in one spot. The Prairie Dog Town Fork of the Red River has carved an 800-foot-deep gorge across the high plains and produced a textbook picture of the physical dynamics that have shaped Texas. The gorge is part of **Palo Duro Canyon State Park** and is located 12 miles east of Canyon on TX Hwy 217. At 16,000 acres, it is one of the largest state parks in Texas. Signs point the way from Canyon.

Stop at the first overlook after the Visitor's Center for an overall look at the canyon. The erosion here has taken place during the last one million years, when that tiny stream down in the bottom of the canyon was much larger. Try to see the canyon in early morning or late afternoon light when the different pinks, reds, blues, and golds of the rocks show best.

The paved road through the park is 8 miles in length. A short distance after reaching the bottom of the canyon, pull into the parking lot on the right designating the trail leading to the Lighthouse. This is a 5-mile trail that takes you to the most famous rock formation in the park; the hiking is easy but it is long, so take a canteen of water. The Lighthouse is a tall sentinel of Trujillo sandstone approximately 225 million years old and is an example of how rock erodes at different rates. It has been left standing while everything around it has washed away. This is also why some parts of the canyon walls are smooth and others are rough and why there are towers and pedestals along the cliffs. For additional information, write Palo Duro

Canyon State Park, Rt. 2, Box 285, Canyon, TX 79015, (806) 488-2227.

It is also possible to view millions of years of geologic history at **Caprock Canyons,** a ruggedly beautiful state park southwest of Palo Duro near the town of Quitaque. Follow I-27 north from Lubbock and exit east on TX Hwy 86 at Tulia. Follow this 29 miles to Silverton, then 19 miles to Quitaque. In Quitaque turn left (north) on FM 1065 and follow it 3 miles to park headquarters.

Once past the headquarters, turn right at Lake Theo, following the signs to the Equestrian Camping Area and other campgrounds. Just before you reach the Equestrian Camping Area, stop at the overlook parking area on the left; this will give you your first look at a virtual wall of 280-million-year-old red sandstone.

Follow the paved road to the left (don't turn in at the Equestrian Camp) and across the South Prong of the Little Red River. Look for mule deer here at the same time you're studying the distant rock formations. Follow the road to the South Prong Tent Camping Area and plan to hike from there along the trail leading to the Primitive Camping Area. Just a short stroll along this trail will show how awesome the forces of nature have been over time.

If you drive eastward on U.S. Hwy 90 between Marfa and Alpine, you'll drive through a 35-million-year-old volcano. Thirteen miles east of Marfa you'll enter Paisano Pass, which was an ancient volcano rim; the caldera of this volcano collapsed inward, so you hardly know the volcano is there. Once in Alpine, look back to the west and you'll see the volcano formation on the horizon.

16

Spring Gobblers

If whitetail deer are the unofficial state animal of Texas, the wild turkey is quickly moving into second place. Texas, like every other state in the continental United States, is experiencing an amazing recovery of the bird Benjamin Franklin once nominated to be America's national symbol.

When the Pilgrims landed at Plymouth Rock, the wild turkey population numbered perhaps as many as 10 million birds, centered primarily in the eastern and southwestern parts of America. By the end of World War II, not quite 350 years later, the population had been reduced to less than 30,000.

Today, however, thanks in large part to sportsmen-funded restoration activities, the wild turkey has been re-established throughout its former range; more than two million birds are present in every state except Alaska. This restoration ranks as one of the most dramatic and successful conservation efforts ever undertaken.

Wild turkeys are uniquely North American; there are no relatives in the Old World. The Aztecs are believed to have been the first to domesticate the bird; old diaries indicate that Cortez took these birds back to Spain, and colonists later brought them back to America. The holiday birds enjoyed at Thanksgiving and Christmas are probably descendants of those turkeys.

For pure wildness, few birds can match the turkey. It has extraordinary hearing and very keen eyesight. Along with these, each wild turkey seems to be born with a compass in its brain; the bird can hear a sound once and walk right to it from half a mile away, and it can remember the exact spot it found corn or acorns a year before.

In March and continuing into April, a tom turkey's instincts turn to love. From his lofty roost on an oak or cypress limb, he gobbles to attract the attention of a hen. It's a quick, coarse but high-pitched, rolling chuckle that once heard is unmistakable. Gobbling normally occurs right around sun-up, and the fewer hens available, the more intense the gobbling activity will be. Turkeys will also gobble at hooting owls, cawing crows, and sometimes a slamming truck door.

Turkeys actually have a distinct language of their own composed not only of gobbling but also of yelps, clucks, purrs, and other sounds. Each has a special meaning, and it is those sounds hunters try to imitate when calling turkeys into camera or shotgun range.

Hens are attracted to the gobbling and once the two are together, an elaborate and spectacular courtship display begins. The tom spreads his tail feathers in a wide fan, puffs out his chest, and begins strutting back and forth in front of his newfound love. His wing feathers drag on the ground, and he starts "drumming" by expelling air from his lungs.

Gobblers are identified by their overall darker feathers, reddish head (hens almost always appear lighter with gray heads), chest beard, and sharp hornlike pro-

When a wild turkey gobbler tries to impress a hen, he puffs out his body, fans his tail, and begins strutting before her. Sportsmen skilled at imitating a hen's call can often lure gobblers quite close.

trusions on the back of their ankles known as spurs. A mature bird will weigh between 15 and 20 pounds.

Growth comes quickly because turkeys don't live very long in the wild. In fact, just being born is a feat, as approximately half of each 12-egg clutch gets destroyed by predators, and half of the hatched poults rarely survive longer than four weeks. The overall annual population turnover is estimated to be as high as 30 percent.

Fortunately, however, wild turkeys have an extremely varied diet, so there is plenty of latitude in their habitat requirements. That's what has allowed them to be re-established so successfully. They eat a wide variety of berries, seeds, nuts, and insects and are mobile enough to forage as much as several miles daily.

Hot Spots

One place wild turkeys can often be seen by casual observers is at the **Kerr Wildlife Management Area** near Hunt. To reach the area, drive 12 miles northwest of Hunt on Ranch Road 1340 to the entrance. This 6,493-acre area offers several driving-tour options, so be sure to pick up a guide booklet at the mailbox near the entrance.

Another area for a possible turkey sighting is **South Llano River State Park,** located 5 miles west of Junction on TX Hwy 377. This park has one of the oldest winter turkey roosting areas in the state. A quiet, careful walk through the park often provides a glimpse of these wary birds.

A third area to consider is the **Hill Country State Natural Area,** located 12 miles south of Bandera on FM 1077. This 5,400-acre tract is extremely primitive but offers excellent hiking trails (also used by equestrians) for game viewing. Walk the trails early in the morning for best results.

17

March Shorttakes

Lost Pines

Unless you're in East Texas, pine trees are hard to find. The state's overall dry climate is much more suitable to oaks and junipers. There is one place, however, where pine trees outnumber the other species, even though the terrain doesn't seem to favor them. It's a 3,500-acre island of loblolly pines left over from the Ice Age, located in **Bastrop State Park** in Central Texas. To reach the park, follow TX Hwy 21 one mile east from Bastrop to the entrance.

When glaciers covered much of North America as far south as Kansas, the climate was much wetter than it is today. At that time, pine trees covered not just the eastern portion of Texas but also the higher Central Texas plateau and into the western basin beyond. The melting of the glaciers signaled a major climatic change that brought far less rainfall. Oaks and other species became dominant except in the eastern part of Texas—and in Bastrop. The reason pines have survived in this 70-square-mile pocket is because the pine tree roots are able to tap into a very shallow underground aquifer that provides all the water they need. Ironically, the pines grow side by side with cedars, oaks, coupons, and other dry-climate species. The pines are particularly noticeable in March before the oaks and other species have leafed out for the spring.

18

A Closer Look: Mountain Lions and Coyotes

Of all the wildlife in Texas, none personifies secrecy, mystery, and pure wildness more than the mountain lion. Easily recognized by all but understood by few, this largest of the North American long-tailed cats has been feared and revered, persecuted and honored since before the first colonists stepped ashore nearly four centuries ago.

If the mountain lion personifies secrecy, however, then the coyote personifies cunning, tenacity, and crafty intelligence. It is the smallest of the North American wolves, and its population actually appears to be expanding in the face of adversity.

The two animals are integral parts of the Texas landscape, and, while their ranges overlap in certain regions, they are as different as night and day. Mountain lions are silent and solitary, inhabiting the most harsh, hard country the Lone Star State has to offer; the coyote is an evening serenader that often lives at the edge of the state's largest cities.

Mountain lions are descendants of the family Felidae, which has been on earth for tens of millions of years. Originally their range extended from the Atlantic to the Pacific and from the Canadian Yukon to the Strait of Magellan; even today they inhabit this long north-south corridor, the most extensive range of any land mammal in the Western Hemisphere.

This is in itself remarkable, for it means that the mountain lion—also commonly known as the panther, cougar, and puma across its range—has adapted not only to the dry, rocky badlands of the Southwest but also to rain forests, high mountains, swamps, and deserts. Mountain lions were described by Columbus after one of his earliest voyages to the New World, by the Spanish explorer Coronado on his expedition across the Southwest in 1540, and by Captain John Smith of the Virginia colony in 1610.

Why, then, has the great cat remained in virtual obscurity? Actually, there are two answers. The first is because mountain lions are shy, reclusive, solitary animals. They are not totally nocturnal, but their senses of sight, hearing, and smell are sharp enough that they can easily stay away from humans, their only real enemy. The second reason is because the big cats spend most of their lives on the move. They are meat eaters and so are most often on the hunt. The size of their hunting territory is often a huge circle 50 to 75 miles in diameter, and a daily movement of 15 to 20 miles through this territory isn't at all unusual.

While mountain lions exist primarily on deer, elk, javelina, and rabbits, their daily hunting movements invariably bring them into contact with ranch livestock, and thus cattle, horses, goats, and pigs at times also become part of their diet. This, of course, has contributed to the animal's reputation and led to intense predator-control measures in many parts of its range.

In Texas there may be more mountain lions than anyone has ever realized. One reason is that sheep and goat herds have declined while deer and javelina have increased. As a result, in 1995 the Texas Parks and

Wildlife Department began a three-year study to learn more about the elusive cats and try to determine their Texas population.

Coyotes occupy the exact opposite end of the wildlife scale. Some scientific studies seem to indicate that litters of pups may actually be larger in areas where the animal is under the greatest stress. Originally, coyotes probably occupied only the western half of North America between the Rockies and the Mississippi River. Today they're found throughout the United States as far north as Alaska and well into Central America.

This expansion has come because of the coyote's ability to adapt to a changing world. Whereas the mountain lion eats only meat, the coyote eats practically anything. Rabbits and rodents are probably its favorite foods, but only until a patch of watermelons, a stand of sweet corn, or even a field of grasshoppers is located. They'll eat berries, cactus, tomatoes, and even your pet's dog or cat food.

Unlike that of most wild animals, the coyote's intelligence seems to transcend pure survival instincts. The animal quickly learns to avoid baited traps, while at the same time it has been known to "adopt" some humans as trusted friends. Coyotes occasionally hunt in pairs, coordinating their efforts just like a well-trained military team, and their will to survive is so strong they'll chew off their own paws to escape a trap.

Weighing only about 25 pounds and standing 24 inches tall at the shoulder, coyotes are best known for their evening serenades, which are commonly heard throughout much of Texas. This "song dog of the prairie," as the coyote is often known, may bark or howl at any time, and biologists who have studied the animal believe the howling is actually a form of communication.

Some calls warn of danger, some assemble other coyotes, and some appear to be made simply because the animal is happy. A lone coyote is often joined by others until the evening is filled with a wild, ancient chorus that rings across the plains and over the hills in a rolling crescendo. Without question, it is one of nature's most enduring symbols.

April

Notes

19

Spring Bluebonnet Trails

Slightly more than a century ago, during the spring of 1886, Mary Taylor Bunton talked her husband into letting her accompany him on a cattle drive from their North Texas ranch along the Chisholm Trail. The young Mrs. Bunton was provided with a buggy, and she followed beside the herd on a hot and often hazardous journey through extremely rugged country. What impressed her most, however, was not the danger but rather the beauty. Specifically, the beauty of wildflowers.

Describing the trip later in her book, *A Bride on the Old Chisholm Trail in 1886,* she wrote, "Wildflowers grew in the greatest profusion everywhere and there were many rare varieties that I had never seen before. ... Sometimes I would fill my buggy and decorate my horses' bridles and harness with the gorgeous blossoms, then I would weave a wreath for my hair and a chaplet of flowers for my shoulders. ... Seated in my flower-bedecked buggy it was easy enough for me to pretend that I was taking part in a grand flower parade."

Although more than 5,000 species of flowering plants are native to Texas, it is likely that at least a few of the flowers Mrs. Bunton enjoyed were bluebonnets, *Lupinus texensis.* There are actually six different species of bluebonnets in the Lone Star State, and taken collectively they are such a strong part of the Texas heritage they were adopted as the state flower in 1901.

Mrs. Bunton was not the first to describe the beautiful blue flowers. Botanists sent from Spain and England as early as the 1820s to collect plant specimens in the New World were both amazed and awed at the vast fields and meadows of bluebonnets that stretched for miles across the rolling hills.

The very same fields become covered today, beginning in mid to late March and usually peaking during the first two weeks of April. Some have described the scene as a time when the sky falls on Texas, while others liken it to a gently rolling sea of the bluest blue. Whatever the description, to see such huge expanses of wildflowers is an unforgettable experience.

The bluebonnet is a legume, which makes it distantly related in some ways to wisteria, peas, and even clover because it returns nitrogen to the ground. It has five petals, and although its color is primarily blue, some pinkish flowers are occasionally found, as are white albinos. Insects readily feed on the flowers, and deer will eat them when nothing else is available, but cattle won't touch them.

Bluebonnets are found in many places besides the open ranchlands. Today, they also grow along hundreds of thousands of miles of Texas roadways, allowing them to be enjoyed by virtually anyone traveling in the state. This is the result of a program started more than 60 years ago when Jack Gubbels, the first landscape architect for the Texas Highway Department (now the Department of Transportation), developed and implemented a plan for roadside beautification. Not only was Texas the first state in America to plant flowers along its roadways, the department has continued the project ever since. Today tons of wildflower seeds are planted along nearly a million miles of Texas highways each year.

In 1965, Congress passed the National Highway Beautification Act, largely through the efforts of Lady Bird Johnson, wife of President Lyndon B. Johnson. Both, of course, were native Texans and used the state as an example of what could be accomplished in other parts of the country.

In 1982, Mrs. Johnson helped establish the National Wildflower Research Center near Austin, and it became so successful that the facility had to move to a new location in 1993. Mrs. Johnson donated the land for the new center as well as helped finance building construction.

Although visual enjoyment is certainly the most obvious benefit of this project, the annual bluebonnet reseeding actually accomplishes several things. The flowers not only help stabilize the soil and replenish nitrogen, they also provide food for a wide variety of wildlife. At the same time, bluebonnets save the Department of Transportation thousands of dollars in mowing and maintenance costs in just the few weeks they are blooming.

Hot Spots

Although there are many driving routes (known as bluebonnet trails) throughout the state, a good place to start is near the city of Burnet, which is known as the Bluebonnet Capital of Texas. Follow TX Hwy 29 west out of Burnet for $3^1/_2$ miles, then turn right (north) on Ranch Road 234 and follow it about 6 miles. Turn left on Graphite Mine Road, which will eventually meet TX Hwy 29. Turn left to return to Burnet.

A variation of this drive will give you different but equally spectacular views of bluebonnets as well as of Lake Buchanan. Follow TX Hwy 29 west and again turn right on RR 234. If you stay on this road, you'll have 15 miles of vistas before it finally dead-ends. You can return via the same route or make the turn on Graphite Mine Road.

If you want to see even more of the Hill Country, simply stay on TX Hwy 29 west all the way to Llano, a distance of about 30 miles. In Llano, turn left (south) on TX Hwy 16 and follow it to Fredericksburg (39 miles). In Fredericksburg turn left (east) on U.S. Hwy 290 and follow it 32 miles to Johnson City, then follow U.S. Hwy 281 north 37 miles to Burnet.

Another beautiful bluebonnet drive leads west from Brenham on U.S. Hwy 290 to Giddings (35 miles), south on U.S. Hwy 77 to LaGrange (20 miles), then north on TX 159 and 237, which will get you back to U.S. 290 in the city of Burton, about 15 miles west of Brenham.

Each April 24, Texas celebrates State Wildflower Day, and many cities have pageants, parades, and other celebrations. A partial listing of cities includes

Mason, Chappell Hill, Keney, Glen Rose, Ennis, and Hughes Springs. The best way to learn what is scheduled is to contact the National Wildflower Research Center, 4801 La Crosse Avenue, Austin, TX 78739, (512) 292-4100. During March, April, and May, the Department of Transportation also has a telephone hotline with information on where bluebonnets are blooming: (800) 452-9292.

20

Where Birds Fall from the Sky

Each spring what few trees there are along the upper Texas coast change color. The color comes not from leaves turning red, gold, and yellow as in the autumn, but from birds. Literally thousands of warblers, orioles, tanagers, grosbeaks, buntings, vireos, and other species give the landscape a spectacular display of living color.

The birds coming to Texas in April and May are known as neotropicals, a term describing birds that migrate from their nesting habitat in the United States and Canada to tropical habitats in Mexico and Central and South America rather than stopping along the Gulf Coast for the winter. Included in this huge category are more than 250 species of small songbirds, and they're the ones that become temporary Texans.

In early March, the birds begin gathering on the Yucatan peninsula in Mexico, resting from flights that may have already brought them a thousand miles. For several weeks they feed heavily to store energy and build up fat reserves, since the most demanding part of their northward migration lies ahead—more than 600 miles across the Gulf of Mexico.

This is what makes the trees and bushes of the upper Texas coast so important; it is the first landfall the birds have after hours of nonstop flying. Although many continue northward for another hundred miles or so before landing, thousands stop at this first opportunity.

The trip might be as short as 12 hours if the migrants can take advantage of strong southerly winds, but several times each spring the birds run into a huge thunderstorm or an unseasonably fierce north wind that makes the trip 24 to 30 hours. Many migrants perish in the Gulf, but those that do reach Texas drop out of the sky totally exhausted.

This is known as a fallout, and it is one of the most unforgettable spectacles in all of ornithology. One tree may have 15 or more different species of warblers, another will be filled with orange and black orioles, scarlet tanagers, and rose-breasted grosbeaks. Even ruby-throated hummingbirds will be present.

Bird migrations have fascinated humankind for hundreds of years, and the migrations of the neotropicals are even more remarkable because of their small size. They are forced to migrate because winter brings an end to their food supply. Between August and October these same birds, many of them in their immature plumage, gather along the Texas coast before making the southern Gulf crossing. It is their return in the spring, however, when they have their brightly colored adult plumage, that draws the most attention. For many observers, the arrival of the neotropicals signals the true beginning of spring and the start of another of nature's wondrous cycles.

High Island

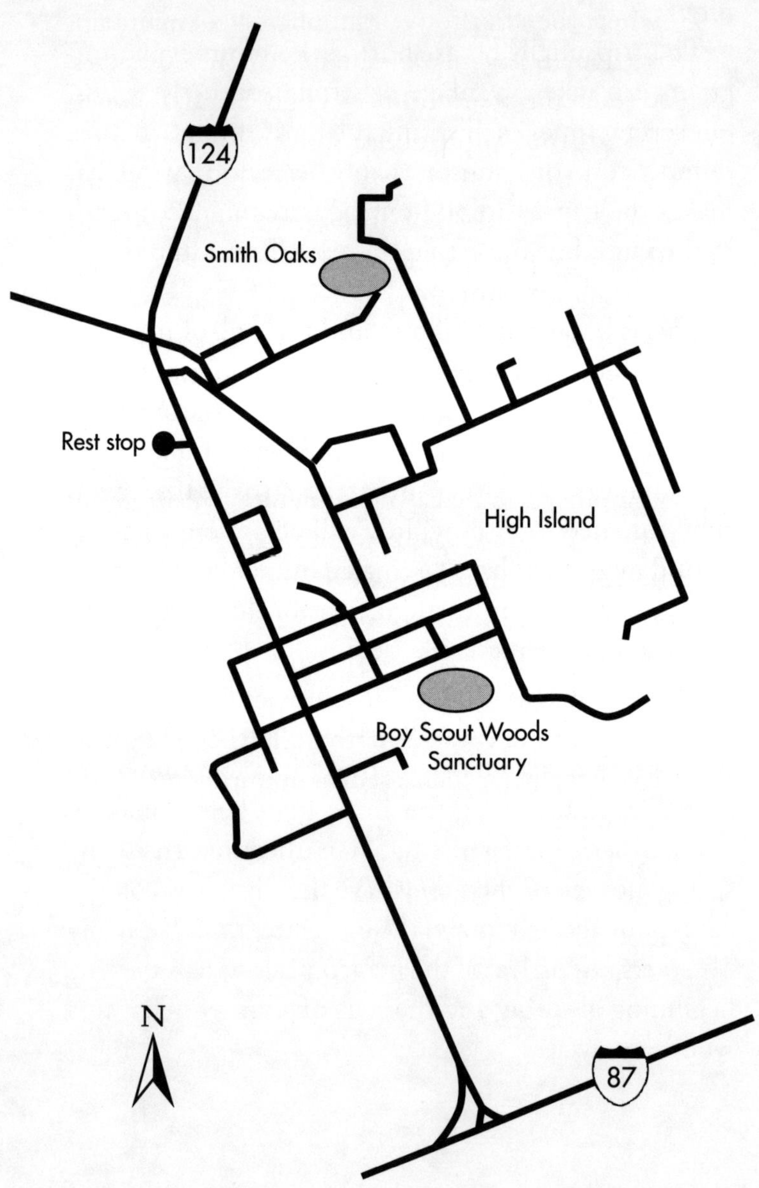
124
Smith Oaks
Rest stop
High Island
Boy Scout Woods
Sanctuary
N
87

Hot Spots

The most famous spot in Texas to see the spring migration and possible fallout is **High Island,** where the Houston Audubon Society maintains two superb sanctuaries totaling about 200 acres. To reach the community of High Island, follow I-10 east from Houston 65 miles to Winnie, then turn south on TX Hwy 124 for 20 miles. The first sanctuary, Smith Oaks, is reached by turning east (left) on Winnie Street on the north side of town and following the signs less than a mile.

To reach Boy Scout Woods Sanctuary continue south on 124 and turn east (left) on Fifth Street and follow the signs. Both areas have trails and boardwalks that lead through a variety of habitats.

Another spot that attracts migrating neotropicals is **Sabine Woods,** a 32-acre sanctuary owned by the Texas Ornithological Society and located approximately 30 miles northeast of High Island. Follow TX Hwy 87 south from Port Arthur to Sabine Pass, then follow it southwest 4 miles. Signs also point the way. More than 30 species of warblers have been identified here during the April migration.

21

White Bass Spawning Runs

One of the rites of spring in Texas is fishing for the white bass, *Morone chrysops.* These popular game fish, which seldom weigh more than three or four pounds, make up for their small size with sheer numbers—hundreds of thousands of them migrate up rivers and streams between January and May in their annual spawning runs. Along the way they feed ravenously, so they're easy to catch, even when fishing from the shore. If you happen to be driving over a bridge and see a lot of cars parked below, you can guess the spawning run is in progress.

White bass, also known as sand bass or sandies throughout much of the state, are closely related to the larger striped bass. In fact, white bass and stripers have been bred in hatcheries to produce a third fish, the hybrid striper, which has characteristics of both fish. All are silvery white with several dark horizontal lines running from the gills to the tail.

The main characteristic everyone loves about the white bass is that throughout its short life (normally three to four years) it is a very active schooling fish. Where there is one white bass, there may be hundreds more. This is true not only during the migratory spawning runs but also during the rest of the year when the fish are commonly found in the larger lakes.

Beginning as early as December in South Texas but not until March or April farther north, white bass begin staging at the mouths of the rivers and major tributaries that feed into the lakes. Then they start moving upstream in huge concentrations that continue for several weeks.

In virtually every instance the fish get stopped by dams, and when they do, they gather in ever-increasing numbers until the conditions are right for spawning. Unlike the largemouth bass that constructs a nest and then guards both eggs and fry, the female white bass sends her eggs out into the open water.

The eggs are fertilized by the male as they settle. Some attach to rocks and gravel, while current and waves begin washing others downstream. Hatching occurs in two to three days, but overall survival is relatively low. Although as many as a million eggs may be laid, only about 20 to 30 percent will usually survive and grow to adulthood.

A century ago white bass were found only in scattered watersheds across the eastern and midwestern regions of America, but today they have spread throughout most of the nation. In Texas the fish were native only to Caddo Lake, but in 1932 biologists took 13 brood fish from Caddo to Lake Lewisville north of Dallas, and now white bass swim in river systems across the state.

The young fry grow rapidly as they feed on zooplankton and other microscopic organisms. Soon their diet begins to include tiny insects and eventually other small fish. In some Texas lakes, "sand bass" grow as much as 11 inches their first year.

White bass fishing usually involves lighter spinning and bait-casting tackle, since the average size of the fish caught is about two pounds. Small 1/8-ounce hair and plastic jigs in white, yellow, and chartreuse are popular lures, as are small silver spoons. At times, small topwater popping lures can also be used.

The limit in Texas is 25 white bass per day, 10-inch minimum size. Some lakes have a 12-inch minimum size limit.

Hot Spots

The Colorado River is one of the state's white bass hotspots, with some of the best fishing taking place at **Colorado Bend State Park.** To reach the park, travel to the small town of Bend, approximately 20 miles southeast of San Saba on FM 580. In Bend follow the signs to the park entrance, located 6 miles south on a gravel road. Many anglers fish from the bank at the campground, while others wade or use float tubes. You can also launch a small boat at the park and fish the 10 miles down the Colorado to Lake Buchanan.

In North Texas, excellent fishing is available on the **Clear Fork of the Brazos River** southwest of Benbrook on U.S. Hwy 377. Follow 377 from Benbrook, and just before entering the small community of Wheatland you'll cross the river. Park on the left; well-worn trails lead downstream to favorite fishing spots.

Still another favorite fishing area is where I-45 crosses **Chambers Creek** in Navarro County between the cities of Ennis and Corsicana. Bank fishing is popular, and you'll usually see several cars parked here during the spring run.

Thousands of white bass are also caught annually in the **Trinity River** north of Lake Livingston. The favorite gathering spot is where TX Hwy 7 crosses the Trinity River about 15 miles west of the city of Crockett. Like the other bridge crossings, there is plenty of parking here on either side of the road.

22

Blooming Cactus

No matter where you go in Texas, you will eventually find a cactus. There are dozens of different species in the state, and they live in the sand, in the rocks, in the mountains, and in the valleys. They belong to the landscape as much as live oak trees and bluebonnets.

Many of the cactus are members of the prickly pear family, which has perhaps as many as 200 species. There is little agreement on how many different prickly pears there are because the cactus hybridizes very easily with other members of its genus.

Regardless of the specific species—some you can tell apart only by the color of their spines—prickly pears are those with the big pancake-flat ears, or pads. Some grow in huge clumps 8 to 10 feet tall, while others are much smaller and stay closer to the ground. Generally speaking, however, where there's one prickly pear, there are others nearby.

And, just as generally speaking, where there is one species of cactus, there are frequently others, particularly in the more arid regions of the state. They range from the tall, slender cholla cactus that looks like a continuous, jointed stem without any leaves, but which, nonetheless, is covered with spines, to the sweet-smelling night-blooming cereus, which flowers only after dark.

In between these are the devil's claw, which grows so low to the ground that the ranchers have nicknamed it the horse crippler, as it is often felt before it is seen; the button cactus, which is even smaller, measuring perhaps an inch tall and half an inch wide; and peyote, the famous hallucinogen used for centuries by Native Americans.

Cactus flowers begin blooming in late spring and continue into early summer, depending on the weather, and turn the desert into an artist's palette of yellows, reds, oranges, and purples. Many flowers will have more than two dozen petals, and a sudden spring rain seems to trigger spontaneous blooming overnight. Botanists believe the mineral content of the soil helps determine flower colors in a particular plant, as there are usually numerous variations in colors around the state.

All cactus are succulents; they store water in their tissues. This is what makes them such valuable food sources for wildlife. The prickly pears, with their wide, easily reached pads, are a favorite. In some parts of Texas as much as 25 percent of a whitetail deer's diet may be prickly pear, and javelina may depend on them for all of their water at certain times of the year.

In most species of cactus, the surface of the plant will feel slightly greasy or waxy to the touch. This is partly how the cactus retains its water, as this coating helps slow evaporation in the heat. The spines do more than protect the plant, too; the shadows they form also help stop evaporation.

While most people today prefer to admire the cactus from a distance, historically the plants have been an important food source for humans as well as wildlife. Both the pads and the flowers of young prickly pear are taken. The flowers, known as tunas, ripen in late summer (this is when they turn deep purple) and can be peeled and eaten like berries, while jelly is made from the flower juice. The pads, which have been found to be high in vitamin C, are cut before the spines start growing and are added to salads, boiled, and even fried.

Hot Spots

Big Bend National Park provides more different cactus species in one location than any other place in the state, as more than 70 species have been recorded here. To reach the park, follow U.S. Hwy 385 south from Marathon. After passing the Persimmon Gap Ranger Station, practically anywhere you look you'll see some type of cactus. Various prickly pear species will immediately become apparent, and many of these are the Englemann prickly pear, the most common of all the prickly pear family. Some of the others will require more searching.

In Dagger Flat (a sign pointing to the left from the main entrance highway points the way) you can look for the blind prickly pear, recognizable because it has no spines. If you don't find it here, look on the cliffs near Boquillas Canyon.

Another resident of Dagger Flat is the brown-flowered cactus, a small, cylindrical "barrel" cactus growing 8 to 10 inches tall. It is particularly abundant in this area and normally has reddish brown flowers. Here you should also find the strawberry cactus, named for its bright red flowers and its large fruit, which is often eaten just like its namesake.

From Dagger Flat the road leading south to Panther Junction begins to climb into the Chisos Mountains. Here you'll find the Chisos prickly pear, which rarely grows higher than two to three feet. It has yellow flowers and long, yellow spines.

Around Rio Grande Village, look for more of the tall Englemann prickly pear, as well as the Chisos pitaya, a cylindrical cactus about a foot tall with white and green flowers.

Anywhere near the canyons and along the river, you should see cane cholla, with its deep purple flowers and yellow fruit; Turk's head cactus, the largest of the barrel cactus, with yellow flowers; and candle cholla, named because it looks like a candelabra with its angular joints.

Normally, cactus begin blooming in Big Bend during the first two weeks of April, and many park visitors go at that time of year just to see the flowers. To make sure you time your visit right, contact the superintendent, Big Bend National Park, TX 79834, (915) 477-2251.

23

April Shorttakes

Blooming Buckeyes

For many nature lovers in Dallas, spring does not officially arrive until the buckeyes bloom along the Texas Buckeye Trail in the **Great Trinity Forest** of south Dallas. The Texas buckeye *(Aesculus glabra arguta)* is a variety of the Ohio buckeye, a medium-sized tree that produces colorful clusters of yellow blossoms between March and May. The tree is known not only for its flowers but also for the slightly offensive odor produced when any of its flowers, leaves, or bark is crushed. To many, the tree is known as the fetid buckeye because of this odor.

The Texas Buckeye Trail winds through the 8,500-acre Great Trinity Forest in Rochester Park, generally paralleling the Trinity River. The trail is 4 miles in length, and the best place to start walking is at the end of Bexar Street. From I-75 (Central Expressway in Dallas) exit east on U.S. Hwy 175, then exit south on Bexar Street and follow it approximately 1 mile until it dead-ends.

24

A Closer Look: Jackrabbits and Other Rabbits

Of all the wildlife common to Texas, none is so often misidentified as the jackrabbit. This long-eared, fast-running resident of the open plains is easily recognized and soon becomes a familiar sight, but it is not a true rabbit at all. It belongs to the family of hares, and its real relatives are generally found in Europe. Texas has several species of true rabbits, including the eastern cottontail, the swamp rabbit or well-known "cane cutter," the Davis Mountains cottontail, and the Audubon cottontail. Of these, the eastern cottontail—most likely the species of Peter Rabbit fame—is the most widespread and well known.

Cottontails are found east of the Rockies from southern Canada to Mexico, in the open range, in the mountains, in the forests, on farms and ranches, and even in quiet neighborhood backyards. Probably the main reason they're so widespread is because their diet is so varied—basically any green plant is food for a cottontail, and when the greenery is gone in winter, they'll eat tree bark and brown grasses. As spring grasses begin to appear, the rabbits become much more visible.

Stories abound about the ability of the cottontail to reproduce, and many of them are true. Someone calculated that in three years one pair of cottontails could have over 10 million descendants. A female can give birth to perhaps 25 to 30 young a year, and half of those will be females capable of breeding within a few months after birth.

What keeps the earth from being overrun with rabbits is the fact that very few live more than a full year. Practically everything that lives in the wild feeds on cottontails, from ants to mountain lions. That's why nature gave rabbits such fertile reproduction capabilities; they're an extremely important part of the food chain.

Although the other rabbits certainly form part of the food chain as well, their role is not as crucial. The swamp rabbits, for example, have only two to three litters annually and usually only two or three young per litter. Likewise, the jackrabbit has fewer and smaller litters. Being true hares, jackrabbit young are born fully furred and with their eyes open. Within minutes after birth they're hopping about, and before too many days pass they're able to match their parents jump for jump at over 40 miles an hour.

Cottontails, on the other hand, are born blind and without fur. They're completely helpless for about a week, and this is certainly when they're most vulnerable to predators. Although cottontails do make a small ground nest (jackrabbits do not) of grasses and fur, it doesn't offer much protection.

The swamp rabbits are a strange mix between jackrabbits and cottontails. They do build nests in logs or stumps, and the young are born fully furred, but they're born blind. They leave the nest in about a week.

In contrast to jackrabbits and cottontails, swamp rabbits like water. Not only do they live in marshy, swampy areas, they are excellent swimmers and do not hesitate to hide in water or use it as an avenue of escape. They do not have webbed feet, as some have said, but they do have an unusually wide foot that aids them in paddling. The name "cane cutter" refers to one of the rabbit's favorite foods, which is cut very distinctly with the animal's sharp incisors.

Two other rabbits in Texas are more closely related to the eastern cottontail than to the swamp rabbit or the jackrabbit. These are the Davis Mountains cottontail, which lives in the juniper and oak forests of the Davis, Guadalupe, and Chisos Mountains; and the Audubon cottontail, whose range extends throughout much of the Rocky Mountain West. Many know it as the desert cottontail or prairie dog rabbit, because it is often found in the plains and prairies near prairie dog towns.

May

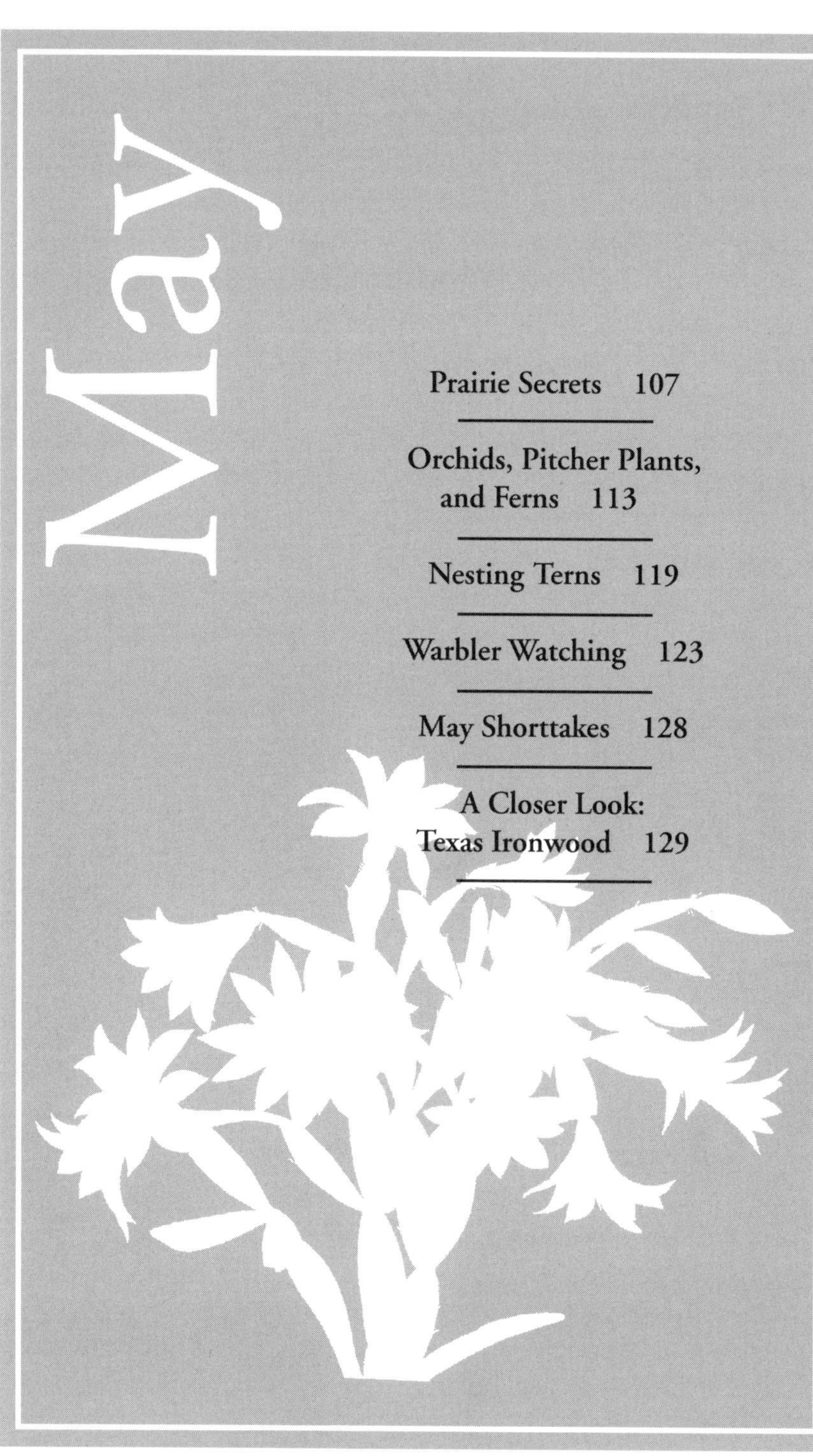

Notes

25

Prairie Secrets

When the first settlers from the East reached the prairie country of the Midwest less than two centuries ago, they could hardly believe their eyes. Instead of the heavily forested slopes of the Appalachian and Cumberland Mountains they had been accustomed to, they now looked at mile after rolling mile of virtually treeless grassland—grasses so tall they nearly swallowed the wagons. It was quickly christened the "sea of grass," and the wagons became prairie "schooners," but few wanted to stop and settle. They felt the land was too poor because there were no trees; it was not until many years afterward that the prairie's secret was realized: This was the richest land in all of North America.

Today the vast prairies have disappeared. Scattered remnants remain in Texas and Oklahoma, but they are only a tiny fraction of the grasslands that once stretched from Texas to Minnesota and across to the eastern slope of the Rocky Mountains. When the prairies were destroyed by settlement, an entire ecosystem was also destroyed.

That ecosystem began some 60 million years ago when the vast ocean that covered much of central North America retreated and the region quickly became forested. But the subsequent uplifting of the Rocky Mountains changed the weather. The high peaks blocked moisture-laden Pacific winds and created what today is known as a "rain shadow"—a region that receives very little rainfall.

Because most trees can live only a short time without water, they soon withered and died. Over eons of time, new plants able to survive without so much water evolved. These were the grasses the pioneers encountered.

It wasn't as if trees didn't try to grow again. They did, but the growing was tough, especially since some of the grasses developed root systems 20 feet deep to soak up any available moisture. Natural fires started by lightning also burned the prairies regularly, stimulating new grasses but further eliminating tree growth.

Scientists believe three types of prairie eventually evolved across the region. These were the short-grass prairie, composed of various blue grasses with shallow root systems, which grew closest to the Rockies; the midgrass prairie of wheat and needlegrass that grew to about four feet in height; and the tallgrass prairie of bluestem, switchgrass, and others that grew as high as 10 or 12 feet because it received the most rain. Texas and Oklahoma had both the tallgrass and midgrass prairies.

Mixed throughout the different grasses were the wildflowers. Black-eyed Susans grew to a height of 15 feet, while coneflower, prairie rose, chickweed, star thistle, Indian blanket, daisy, and dozens of others produced a carpet of wildly mixed colors. In all, the prairies probably produced as many as 500 different plant species.

The bird and mammal populations were equally as varied. The largest were the bison, which at one time numbered in the millions; in 1872 buffalo steak was just a penny a pound (today it's closer to $10 a pound) because the animals were so plentiful. Elk, antelope, rabbit, fox, prairie dogs, owls, hawks, wild turkeys, quail, and hundreds more joined them.

Even today on the few remaining tracts, the spring and summer months provide an enchanting glimpse of the prairie past. The flowers still bloom in profusion, the grass waves in the afternoon breezes, and the buffalo roam. In spring, the prairie awakens from its winter slumber and sparkles with life.

The end of the prairies came when the cattlemen discovered the nutritional value of the grasslands for their stock. Here, a steer could gain as much as three pounds a day eating big bluestem. At the same time, John Deere's Prairie Queen steel plow made its appearance and changed the prairies once and for all.

By the beginning of the 20th century the prairie land had been settled and fenced, and two decades later it was practically worn out. With the elimination of the grasses, the sandy soil blew away in the wind. The once hopeful dreams of settlers blew away with it, as thousands of farms were abandoned during the 1920s and 30s.

During the Depression years the Roosevelt administration bought back many of those farms, re-established native grasses, filled the gullies and washes to stop erosion, and planted trees to break the wind. In Texas, some of the farms later came under the administration of the U.S. Forest Service and became the Caddo, LBJ, Rita Blanca, and Black Kettle National Grasslands. In Oklahoma, the Nature Conservancy purchased the 30,000-acre Barnard Ranch near Pawhuska in 1989 and administers it today as the Tallgrass Prairie Preserve, where the total prairie ecosystem is gradually being re-established.

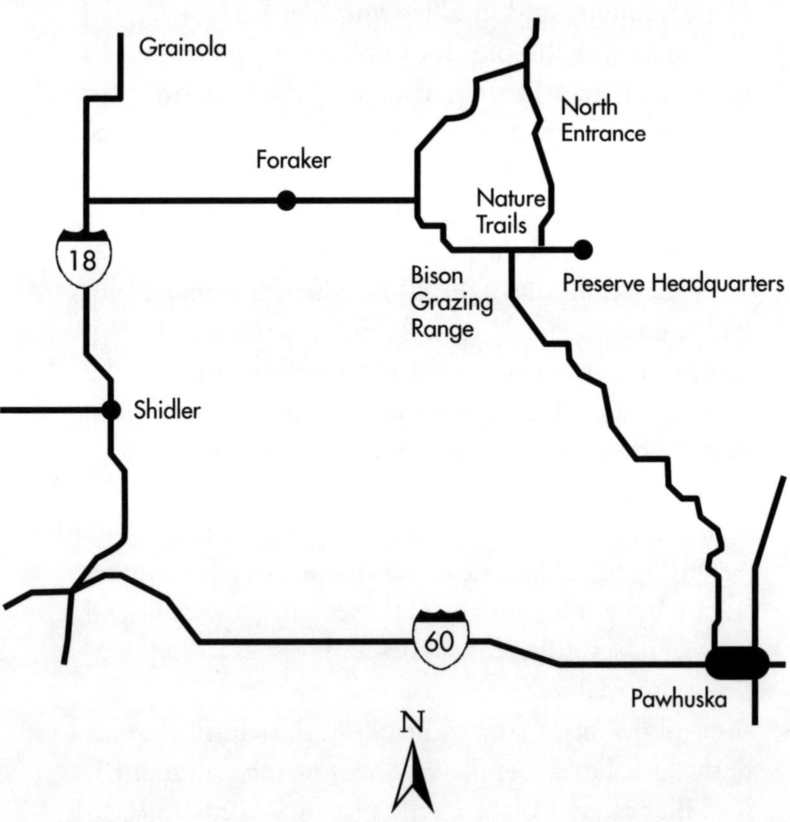
Tallgrass Prairie Preserve
Grainola
North
Entrance
Foraker
Nature
Trails
18
Bison
Grazing
Range
Preserve Headquarters
Shidler
60
Pawhuska
N

Hot Spots

To reach the **Tallgrass Prairie Preserve,** drive north on Osage Avenue out of Pawhuska, Oklahoma; this becomes the Tallgrass Prairie Preserve Drive and enters the preserve from the south 8 miles after leaving Pawhuska. This is a rough gravel road that leads first beside the bison grazing range; 400 head are present now, but the number will eventually increase to 2,000. Follow the signs to preserve headquarters and then continue on the long loop through the preserve. Four parking pullouts offer short trails leading into the tallgrass; a 2-mile nature trail has also been constructed near the headquarters.

May marks the peak of the spring flower blooming season, so take an identification book and look for different species along the various trails. All offer easy, casual walking. It's also a good time to see many of the 300 species of birds that have been identified here, including greater prairie chickens, which may still be booming.

The Caddo, LBJ, Rita Blanca, and Black Kettle National Grasslands are not as dramatic as the Tallgrass Prairie Preserve because they are composed of separate tracts mixed among private land holdings. They are also leased for cattle grazing, and in the case of the Caddo and LBJ Grasslands, the landscape has been modified considerably through the planting of trees.

Caddo National Grassland is located just northeast of Bonham; U.S. Hwy 82 between Paris and Bonham gives good windshield views of what the original prairie may have looked like. The **LBJ National Grassland** is located northwest of Dallas near Decatur off U.S. Hwy 81/287. For specific locations of the various tracts, contact the USDA Forest Service, 2000 South College (FM 730 South), Decatur, TX 76234, (817) 627-5475.

The **Rita Blanca** and **Black Kettle National Grasslands** are located in the Panhandle; Rita Blanca is north of Dalhart in Dallam County, and Black Kettle is in Hemphill County near Canadian. For information and maps detailing these areas, contact the USDA Forest Service, Southwestern Region, Federal Building, 517 Gold Avenue, SW, Albuquerque, NM 87102, (505) 476-3300.

26

Orchids, Pitcher Plants, and Ferns

Every so often, nature's road map seems to get scrambled. Trees, shrubs, and wildlife indigenous to one environment strangely bump into trees, shrubs, and wildlife indigenous to a totally different environment. When it happens 10 times within the space of a few miles, as it does in the Big Thicket National Preserve in East Texas, the result is nothing short of amazing. It is unique in the world.

Four primary ecosystems meet here—southeastern swamp, southwestern desert, eastern forest, and central plain—and together they have created nearly a dozen ecologically distinct vegetation communities. This unusual combination has produced 85 species of trees; 60 different shrubs; and 1,000 flowering plants, including 26 different ferns, 20 different orchids, and four insect-eating plants. And they're growing virtually side by side.

May is a good month to discover some of these botanical oddities, because the orchids and many of the other flowering plants are generally in bloom, and the weather is often still cool enough to keep day hiking enjoyable. Throughout the 86,000 acres of the Big Thicket, there are nine walking and hiking trails varying in length from 1/4 mile to 18 miles.

To many, orchids are not only the jewel of the Big Thicket, they are the jewel of all flowering plants. Always living in harmony with various fungi, orchids are extremely slow growing, produce only a few seeds, and flower only after years of maturation.

Strangely, none of the Big Thicket orchids is an epiphyte which grows on trees; all take root directly in the moist soil. Among the nearly two dozen orchids identified in the Big Thicket are the grass pink, southern coral root, orange-fringed orchid, and rose pogonia, all of which are fairly easy to identify. The swamp pink, for example, grows to a height of nearly four feet, with pale pink flowers nearly two inches wide.

Far more common and easier to find are the carnivorous pitcher plants, which supplement their diet with flies and other insects. They have evolved because of the poor soil; the nonporous clay drains poorly and the standing water leaches out nutrients. To survive, the plants have developed different methods of trapping their prey.

The pitcher plants can usually be identified by their long, funnel-shaped leaves. Nectar on the outside of the leaves near the funnel opening attracts the insects; once the insects are inside the funnel, special downward-pointing hairs prevent escape. The insects fall down the funnel to the base of the plant where they are digested.

Another type of carnivorous plant, the sundew, traps its victims by secreting a sticky nectar on its leaves. Once an insect lands, it becomes stuck and unable to escape.

Ferns are extremely common in many parts of the Big Thicket, growing not only on the moist shade beneath the towering hardwoods but also in some of the open meadows in the bright sun. Although ferns have variously shaped leaves and root systems like other flowering plants, they do not produce any flowers themselves. Instead, they reproduce through spores, which actually makes them more closely related to mushrooms.

Among the more common ferns in the Big Thicket are the southern lady fern, cinnamon fern, netted chain fern, and bracken fern. One or more of these, as well as some others, are present along all of the walking trails. The best way to identify them is usually through the arrangement of their leaves.

The question, of course, is how did this huge diversification occur? As with so much of Texas, the answer lies in prehistoric times when the Gulf of Mexico covered this part of the state. Each time the Gulf rose and fell during the melting of the Ice Age glaciers, it left behind various layers of sediments that over time became different soil types.

The northern part of the Big Thicket, for example, is much drier than the southern part. When the Ice Age ended, those plants that had been pushed southward by the glaciers found soil and climate conditions agreeable and thus mixed with those species already present.

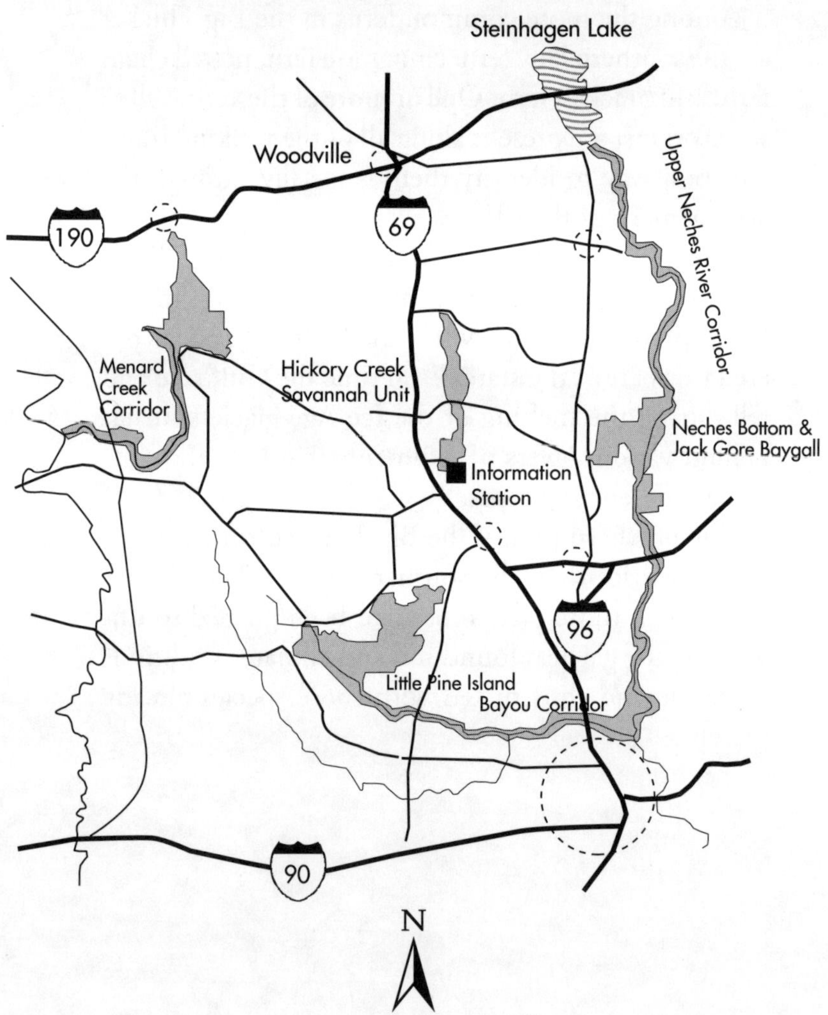
Orchid Hunting in Big Thicket
Steinhagen Lake
Woodville
Upper Neches River Corridor
190
69
Menard
Creek
Corridor
Hickory Creek
Savannah Unit
Neches Bottom &
Jack Gore Baygall
Information
Station
96
Little Pine Island
Bayou Corridor
90
N

Hot Spots

To reach the **Big Thicket National Preserve,** drive south from Woodville or north from Beaumont on U.S. Hwy 69/287. To reach the information station, continue 7 miles north of Kounze on U.S. Hwy 69/287 and turn right on FM 420, then follow this 2 miles. The problem in visiting the Big Thicket is that there are 12 separate, unconnected units rather than the one contiguous unit, so you'll have to decide which one to visit, or simply plan several return trips.

The Kirby Nature Trail is located at the information center, and it's a good place to get a feel for the Big Thicket. It's less than 2 miles in length, basically flat, and leads through several distinct plant communities. You'll see beech, oak, magnolia, cypress, and pine trees as well as Christmas, royal, and netted chain ferns.

One of the better places to find orchids is along the Sundew Trail in the Hickory Creek Savannah Unit. To reach this trail, continue northward on U.S. Hwy 69/287 to FM 2827. Turn left for 1/2 mile, then turn left again at the Hickory Creek Savannah sign and follow this dirt road another 1/2 mile to the parking lot on the right. The trail is easy to follow and offers good viewing of both wildflowers and carnivorous plants.

Pitcher plants and sundews are also easy to find along the Pitcher Plant Trail in the Turkey Creek Unit. To reach the trailhead, continue north on U.S. Hwy 69/287 from FM 2827 to the community of Warren and turn right on FM 1943. Follow the signs 6 miles to the trailhead. This 1/4-mile trail and boardwalk leads into a wetland savannah where both plants are common.

It is also possible to view portions of the Big Thicket by canoe, which is especially pleasant in the spring if rain hasn't made the water too high on the Neches River, Little Pine Island Bayou, or Village Creek. For information, contact the Big Thicket National Preserve, 3785 Milam, Beaumont, TX 77701, (409) 839-2689.

27

Nesting Terns

Wherever gulls are found along the Texas coast, they are usually accompanied by flocks of smaller, more acrobatic birds that, on the whole, appear much more sophisticated and better behaved. Easily distinguished by their smaller size, forked tails, and the fact that they are constantly flying rather than soaring, these are the terns.

Of the 18 species found throughout the United States, six generally begin nesting this month along the Texas coast. They include the endangered least tern, as well as Caspian, royal, sandwich, Forster's and gull-billed terns. Four others, the roseate, sooty, black, and common terns are migrants and less often seen.

Terns are closely related to the gulls, and, while they are quite different in appearance, the birds do share some common characteristics. Both live and nest in large colonies along the Texas coast and nearby marshes; both eat a variety of foods including small saltwater fish and shrimp; and both are quite vocal.

The similarities pretty well end there. Gulls are good swimmers, but terns are not; their webbed feet are too small to propel them for very long. Terns are much stronger flyers than gulls, however. One species, the Arctic tern, is actually one of the migration champions of the bird world, traveling from its summer-nesting grounds in Alaska to its winter habitat in the Antarctic, a round trip of well over 20,000 miles.

Considering the way terns construct their nests, it's a wonder any ever hatch, much less grow strong enough to make such a migration. Most tern nests aren't even nests but simply small depressions in the ground. Some species may line the depression with twigs or mosses, but others don't do anything. As a result, eggs get eaten by gulls and other predators, stepped on or driven over by careless humans, and even washed away by high tides.

Some believe terns survive by sheer numbers, nesting in colonies that often number in the thousands and that frequently include additional species like black skimmers, gulls, and others. Egg laying can begin as early as April and continue into June; the eggs hatch in about three weeks and the young begin flying four to five weeks later. If the original clutch of eggs is destroyed, terns may or may not lay a second time but never a third.

At first glance all terns seem to look alike. They're basically white with black head caps. One key to identifying them is often the bill color, which may be red, orange, black, yellow, or a combination of those colors. The sandwich tern, for example, has a black bill tipped in yellow, while the Forster's tern has an orange-red bill with a black tip.

Terns are easy to distinguish from gulls because not only are they smaller and more streamlined, but they also have much narrower wings and sharply forked tails. These are what give the bird its speed and agility in the air; it's common to see them hover 15 to 20 feet above the water as they study a small fish near the surface, then dive head first into the water to capture that fish.

Hot Spots

One place to see nesting terns, along with many other species of nesting waterbirds, is **Pelican Island** near Galveston. In Galveston, follow 51st Street across the Pelican Island Bridge and continue past the Texas A&M–Galveston campus on the right. Turn left on Bradner Street, the first paved road beyond the campus, and follow it less than a mile to the end.

From there, plan to walk the quarter mile to the levee; birds will be nesting on the far side. Don't walk beyond the levee, and certainly don't drive beyond it, because of the disturbance it will cause.

Another tern nesting site that can be viewed from a distance is along the sand flats at **San Luis Pass** approximately 20 miles south of Galveston. Follow FM 3005 from Galveston to the San Luis Pass bridge, but don't cross it. Instead, park on the side of the road and walk north across the dunes and marsh to West Bay. The birds often lay their eggs on the sand and shells here. Again, walk carefully and stay at least 200 feet away from the nesting birds.

At the opposite end of Galveston Island, **Big Reef Nature Park** also offers a chance to see nesting terns. To reach the park, follow Seawall Boulevard eastward out of Galveston to the end, then turn right on Apfell Road. The refuge is located less than 1/2 mile down Apfell Road, on the left.

One of the last places one would expect to see an endangered species like the least tern nesting is in the middle of an urban area, but between May and August the birds lay eggs and raise their young in downtown Tulsa, Oklahoma. They use two small, largely barren islands in the Arkansas River, which flows through the city.

Located between 11th and 21st Streets and Riverside Drive, this particular part of the river is known as Zinc Lake. The best viewing is probably from the 11th Street bridge (which includes pedestrian lanes) crossing the river. Access to the islands themselves is not permitted during the nesting season. This entire area is part of a 650-acre park administered by the River Parks Authority of Tulsa.

28

Warbler Watching

Each spring the Texas forests and thickets come alive with flashes of yellow, orange, and red as warblers arrive from their wintering grounds in Central and South America. Of the 56 species of warblers found in North America, more than 30 can be found in Texas, and one, the golden-cheeked warbler, is found nowhere else.

These diminutive birds, nearly all of them smaller than the common sparrow, comprise the second largest family of North American songbirds (only finches are more numerous) and are as well known for their songs as for their colors. For example, the hooded warbler's high, quick, often repeated two-note call, once recognized, is easily identified and remembered.

The majority of warblers are insect eaters, although some supplement this diet with small fruits and berries. Thus, most warblers are seen flitting from limb to limb or along the ground quickly and actively as they chase down their food. It is this diet that forces them to migrate to the warmer climates each winter and puts them into the broad category of birds known as neotropicals. Among the many warblers that migrate through Texas are the yellow-throated, bay-breasted, and Kentucky warblers.

Upon their return to the United States each spring, starting as early as March and continuing into May, some warblers fly as far north as the Canadian provinces. Many, however, remain in Texas, where they nest. The nests are as varied as the birds that make them. Most are quite small and well hidden, but one may be in a hedge just above the ground, another in a hollow stump, and still another 80 feet up in an oak.

Of special interest to Texas birders is the golden-cheeked warbler, which nests in limited habitat in the Texas Hill Country. Because its habitat—mature Ashe juniper (commonly called cedar)—is constantly being bulldozed for grazing pastures or construction, the bird has been put on the threatened list. This warbler makes its nests exclusively from strips of shaggy bark it pulls from these trees.

The golden-cheeked warbler's name describes its primary marking. While its back, throat, neck, sides, and crown are black, its cheeks and sides of its neck are bright yellow. Another help in identification is that this is one of the warbler species with two distinct white bars on the wings; some warblers have them and some do not.

Nesting takes place between April and June, and the birds try to claim a territory several acres in size. While the female incubates, the male stays nearby and makes his presence known through song. The eggs hatch in less than two weeks, and both parents share feeding duties. Banding studies have determined that many birds return to the same nesting area each spring.

During nesting, the female golden-cheek often unknowingly becomes a surrogate mother for the brown-headed cowbird, which lays its eggs in the nests of other birds. Even after hatching, the warblers continue to take care of the extra fledgling until it finally leaves to join other cowbirds. Warblers are not the only species that help raise cowbirds, but some believe this leads to increased nest failures among smaller birds.

Hot Spots

Golden-cheeked warblers are reliably seen in **Pedernales Falls State Park** near Johnson City. From Johnson City, drive east on FM 2766 for 7 miles to the park entrance on the left. The best viewing spots are along the Hill Country Nature Trail near the campground; take the paved loop road through the camping area until you see signs and the parking pullout for the nature trail.

Golden-cheeked warblers are also present near the Pedernales River waterfalls. Follow the main park road signs pointing the way to the falls, and park in the designated area. The short, easy walking trail to the river leads through mature Ashe juniper forest and has several short spur trails, so look for the warblers anywhere in this area. For information, contact the park at Rt. 1, Box 450, Johnson City, TX 78636, (210) 868-7304.

Meridian State Park also offers good chances to see the endangered golden-cheeked warbler. To reach the park, take TX Hwy 22 west from Meridian 3 miles to the entrance. Look for warblers in the woods near the campground and along several nature trails looping out of the campground directly across from park headquarters. Special warbler-watching activities are usually conducted here in late March by park personnel. For information contact the park at Box 188, Meridian, TX 76665, (817) 435-2536.

More than 35 species of warblers have been identified in the spring at **Sea Rim State Park** on the upper Texas coast. To reach the park, take TX Hwy 87 south from Port Arthur to Sabine Pass, then continue west on 87 for 10 miles to the entrance on the left. A long boardwalk leading from the campground is the best place to see warblers.

If you have a canoe, plan to take it to Sea Rim, as a second part of the park known as the Marshlands Unit (on the right off Hwy 87 just before the main park entrance) is accessible only by boat. Many other species of birds will also be seen here, as well as along the Gulf beach. For information, contact the park at P.O. Box 1066, Sabine Pass, TX 77655, (409) 971-2559.

29

May Shorttakes

Texas Tortoises

Only four species of tortoises live in North America, and one of them, the Texas tortoise *(Gopherus berlandiere),* is unique to the Lone Star State. It inhabits much of South Texas but is most often seen in May in the lower Rio Grande Valley in Cameron, Hidalgo, and Willacy counties, where it survives in areas unsuitable for agriculture. Rarely exceeding seven inches in length, the Texas tortoise takes 10 years or more to reach sexual maturity, and mortality is high for both eggs and young. Only one clutch of one to five eggs is produced annually, but those are deposited in several locations in an effort to escape predation.

This tortoise differs from its relatives in that even though it has a fairly well-defined home territory, it does not dig a burrow. Instead, it prefers to take up nightly residence underneath the prickly spines of a convenient cactus. That same cactus also provides part of the tortoise's diet, along with other vegetation. Look for the Texas tortoise at **Bentsen–Rio Grande Valley State Park** west of Mission. One or more is usually in residence fairly close to park headquarters, and others can be seen near the campgrounds.

30

A Closer Look: Texas Ironwood

Throughout much of Texas, especially the western half from the Hill Country southward and then across the Trans Pecos, one tree frequently seems to dominate the landscape. It is a thorny and often scrawny hardwood with a forked and twisted trunk best known for its use as a fuel for barbecue. It is, of course, the mesquite, *Prosopis glandulosa torrey.*

The trees are native to Texas and Mexico and first appear in history at the time of the Aztecs. The name *mesquite* is actually an adaptation from the Aztec name *Mizquitl.* Botanists have identified approximately 30 species of trees and shrubs in the mesquite genus, five of which grow in North America. All are pretty much the same in that they are relatively small and have thorns. Contrary to what many ranchers believe, the tree is not a heavy water drinker, and, in fact, it quickly replenishes the soil with nitrogen. Mesquite is also an important food source for several species of wildlife, including deer and javelinas.

The Aztecs, as well as the Indians and Mexicans who followed them, used the leaves and bark for a variety of medicinal purposes, to cure everything from indigestion to wounds. The gum was used to make glue and dye, and the beans formed an important part of the everyday diet since they could be eaten straight from the tree or made into breads and jellies.

As the cattle industry spread across Texas, cattlemen cut mesquite relentlessly to clear land for grazing. The hard, rot-resistant tree trunks were used as fence posts, spokes for wagon wheels, and even furniture. The original beams in the Alamo were cut from mesquite, and a San Antonio street (Houston Street) was paved with blocks of mesquite wood. The strength and quality of the wood is what led to its local name, Texas ironwood.

Today, the best-known use of mesquite is as a fuel for cooking, since it burns with an extremely hot flame and very little smoke. Restaurants throughout the nation advertise their use of mesquite in an attempt to attract customers familiar with the aromatic flavor the wood imparts.

June

Notes

31

Black Skimmers

"It is a pleasure to sit and watch as they quarter back and forth over the same ground again and again, cutting the smooth surface of the water with their razor-like bills, scaling, wheeling, and turning like giant swallows, silently engrossed in their occupation for which they are so highly specialized." That is how the noted naturalist Arthur Cleveland Bent described the black skimmer *(Rynchops nigra),* one of the most interesting of all the summer birds found along the Texas coast. It is the only bird in which the lower part of the bill is distinctly longer (perhaps as much as a third) than the upper part, and it is this specialization that makes the black skimmer so fascinating to watch.

When it feeds, the bird literally "skims" over the water with its longer lower mandible cutting the surface. Upon finding a small minnow, shrimp, or crustacean, the upper mandible quickly closes and the bird throws back its head and swallows—all without missing a wing beat.

The birds are often seen feeding in flocks, and it's a performance comparable to any stage ballet. The skimmers glide and turn in perfect unison as they cut back and forth across the water. Generally, they feed later in the afternoon and into the evening when shallow water tends to be calmer, but this is not always the case.

You'll also see skimmers feeding during the incoming tide, a characteristic, no doubt, that earned them the nickname of "flood gulls."

Black skimmers were once thought to be closely related to gulls and terns because all three species often nest in close proximity, but in recent years the skimmers have been recognized as a separate species. There are just three in the world: the black skimmer of North and South America, the African skimmer, and the Indian skimmer. The black skimmer is the largest of the three, usually measuring 16 to 20 inches in length, its long, pointed wings spanning as much as 50 inches. Overall coloration is basically black above and white below, with a red bill with a black tip.

The birds nest on beaches, sandbars, and islands along the Gulf coast and up the Atlantic as far as Massachusetts. Normally, four to five eggs are laid in late spring and early summer in shallow depressions in the sand. Curiously, the lower mandible of the bill is the same length as the upper in young birds and does not begin growing longer until the skimmers are nearly full grown.

Even though its toes are slightly webbed, you'll rarely see a black skimmer swimming and never see it dive. Instead, you'll be enthralled just like Bent was, watching it skim back and forth across the shallow water, its lower bill slicing the surface as it searches for a meal.

Hot Spots

Two of the best places to see black skimmers are on Galveston Island and the Bolivar Peninsula southeast of Houston. These are two of the premier birding areas of Texas, and many other species will undoubtedly be seen as well, depending on the season.

To reach Galveston Island, follow I-45 south from Houston to Galveston. Exit on TX Hwy 87 east and follow it to FM 3005. Follow FM 3005 approximately 6 miles west to **Galveston Island State Park.** Look for black skimmers along the beach or follow the main park road back to West Bay, where the birds also feed. The nature trails leading to Oak and Buttererrowe Bayous may also provide views of black skimmers. Special observation structures are located on each trail.

To reach the **Bolivar Peninsula,** follow I-45 south of Houston to Galveston and turn east on TX Hwy 87. Continue on Hwy 87 and follow the signs to the free ferry located 5 miles away. The ferry takes less than 15 minutes to cross the 3 miles to the Bolivar Peninsula. Follow TX 87 north 8/10 mile to the intersection with Loop 108. The road to the right is Rettilon Street. Turn here and drive to the beach, then go south on the hard-packed sand for another 8/10 mile to **Bolivar Flats Shorebird Sanctuary** (a sign marks the area), where skimmers and other species abound.

Black skimmers are also found farther north on Bolivar Peninsula near the town of Gilchrest. Continue north on 87 and cross the bridge at Rollover Pass, then turn left on any of the roads; it's less than a mile to East Galveston Bay, where skimmers, egrets, herons, terns, and gulls are common.

32

Rafting Wild Canyons

"You go south from Fort Davis until you come to the place where the rainbows wait for the rain, and the big river is kept in a stone box, and the water runs uphill, and the mountains float in the air, except at night when they go away to play with other mountains." This colorful description of what is now Big Bend National Park, reportedly penned many years ago by a Mexican cowboy, paints a surprisingly accurate description of what is certainly one of the most fascinating parts of Texas. Although the park has many outstanding features, it is the deep canyons of the Rio Grande that provide its cornerstone.

A summer float through Santa Elena, Mariscal, and Boquillas Canyons is not a high-adventure whitewater trip of crashing waves and threatening falls (although there are stretches of Class II, III, and IV rapids). Instead, it is an adventure of the imagination, a chance to see the dynamics of a river through millions of years, to touch rocks where dinosaurs walked, to feel the pulse of a time so long ago it is otherwise incomprehensible.

To many, the most dramatic of the three canyons is Santa Elena, where sheer rock walls soar 1,500 feet above the river for much of its 9-mile length but are only 50 feet apart at top and bottom—the "stone box" described by the vaquero. It is also the first canyon to be encountered on a river float in the park, and at first glance it looks mysterious and ominous as the river disappears into its depths.

The country upriver is harsh and rugged and mountainous, but it is open. Wandering coyotes leave their tracks on sandbars, and wrens flit back and forth between the cactus. Sometimes a Mexican black hawk will utter its hoarse hunting cry while soaring overhead. But in Santa Elena there are few sandbars, and the sky is reduced to a narrow blue ribbon the hawks shun. Save for the echoing rush of water as it compresses around fallen boulders in a place called the Rock Slide (up to Class IV at high water levels), the canyon is largely silent.

To understand the story of Santa Elena is not easy. The limestone walls date back more than 100 million years, and the river was already flowing before that. What occurred was a series of earthquakes, dozens of them over millions of years, in which the limestone was uplifted.

With each uplift, the Rio Grande continued its endless drive to the sea, cutting an inch at a time. The uplifts did not raise the limestone the same way each time, either. Sometimes one end went up while the other dropped or perhaps shifted sideways. Thus, the layers of stratification within the canyon often tilt in the opposite direction from the river's flow, creating the startling illusion the water is flowing uphill.

Here, perhaps more dramatically than anywhere else, it is possible to actually sense the warp in time, to feel what the earth was like when it was young. Even the muddy-brown water looks old. It glides through the canyon slowly and silently, as if knowing its work will never be finished.

In Mariscal the walls are higher, but the canyon itself is shorter. Now it becomes evident that the Rio Grande was not always as placid as it appears today. In the distant past this was a much more wet land and the river was stronger, tearing its way through the limestone just as rains wore down the surrounding mountains.

It is difficult for a non-geologist to totally understand a process of erosion this massive; the geologic clock goes so far back scientists describe time in epochs, periods, and eras instead of years. Just consider that the processes that shaped the Rio Grande canyons began before the dinosaurs reached their dominance and continued long after their demise.

This erosion is most noticeable in Boquillas Canyon, which can be reached by automobile. Even though the walls reach 1,200 feet high, time and weather have worn them into sloping banks in many places. Huge sandbars show how high the river has been in the past.

While a float through any of the three canyons will provide plenty of time for this perspective in geologic history, one cannot fail to notice another of nature's attractions here: light. It bounces and ricochets off the canyon walls like a symphony throughout the day. There are reds and golds, browns and grays, and even blacks between dawn and dusk. This, perhaps, is what the vaquero meant when he wrote about the rainbows waiting for the rain.

Hot Spots

Although some float and paddle the Rio Grande canyons on their own, it is generally better to travel with a commercial outfitter because there are rapids, and once a canyon is entered, there is no way out except by continuing downriver. Rental equipment, however, is available in Lajitas on the western side of the park. Backcountry camping and river permits are required and are available free from park offices.

The basic Santa Elena float is 20 miles, and most outfitters like to make it over two days, camping at the entrance to the canyon. The Mariscal float is 10 miles and has Class II and III rapids in several areas; the Boquillas Canyon float is normally 33 miles, and there is only one rough spot with Class II or III rapids. This is usually a two-day float, and there are ample places to go ashore for off-river exploring.

Although these three canyons are the best known because of their location within **Big Bend National Park,** the Rio Grande offers a longer and much more remote stretch of whitewater know as the **Lower Canyons.** The commercial float is 83 miles and takes seven days; this part of the Rio Grande has been classified as a national wild and scenic river, and the trip is regarded as one of the premier wilderness floats in the Southwest.

Among the outfitters offering Big Bend and Lower Canyons trips are Far Flung Adventures (P.O. Box 377, Terlingua, TX 79852, (915) 371-2489); Big Bend River Tours & Adventures (Box 317, Lajitas, TX 79852, (800) 545-4240); and Outback Expeditions (P.O. Box 229, Terlingua, TX 79852, (915) 371-2490). Most require rafters to bring only their own sleeping bags and personal items; waterproof bags are provided.

33

Summer Whitetails

Of all the big game animals in North America, the most popular by far is the whitetail deer. Adjectives such as graceful, elegant, and intelligent apply to the whitetail. It also happens to be the most numerous big game animal; biologists estimate there are perhaps 15 million head in the United States, with as many as four million in Texas.

Summer is an excellent time to study these interesting animals because both bucks and does are in the midst of transition. The females either have just given or are about to give birth, and the bucks are rapidly growing new antlers. In a few months, their lifestyles will change completely.

Starting in late spring and continuing into the summer in some regions—approximately $6^1/_2$ months after breeding—does give birth to one or two fawns. These young deer weigh only about five pounds and are extremely weak for several days, but within a week or so they're able to move around quite easily.

As part of nature's protection plan, baby fawns have no scent that would give them away to predators. Thus, the mother is able to lead them to a hiding place in grass or brush, then move away to forage. In addition to being scentless, the young fawn is born with a remarkable camouflage coloration of brown with white spots that helps in its concealment.

Gradually, the fawns become more mobile and begin to follow their parent. Some will remain with her throughout the winter, and others will gradually move away by themselves before winter. The female fawns born in early spring may actually breed their first autumn.

While the does are busy raising the young, the bucks are growing new antlers. The previous antlers may have been shed as early as January in some parts of Texas, and new growth begins almost immediately. By June the new antlers are well formed but covered in what is known as velvet, a soft membrane filled with blood vessels. At this time, the antlers are quite soft and can still be easily damaged.

There are many misconceptions about antler growth and development during the lifetime of a buck. Basically, the size of the antlers depends on genetics, the age of the deer, and the quality of its diet. Normally, a deer will follow a gradual progression to eight antler points in three years. Well-fed deer with a strong genetic background may reach eight points in as little as two years, and others may take four years. A few never grow that many points.

By September the antlers have stopped growing and become hard and the velvet is shed. It begins to peel away, and the bucks help the process by rubbing the antlers against limbs and shrubs. In a few days, the task is usually complete.

The deer are especially easy to see around June because they're often in small groups and show none of the animosity toward each other that they'll start to exhibit in October and November.

Hot Spots

Inks Lake State Park near Burnet offers an excellent chance to see whitetails this month, especially early and late each day. To reach the park, follow TX Hwy 29 west from Burnet for 7 miles, then turn left (south) on Park Road 4 and follow this 3 miles to park headquarters. You'll probably see deer along this road before you reach the park entrance, and they're also common around the campground.

Another excellent viewing area is **Possum Kingdom State Park** near Caddo. To reach the park take U.S. Hwy 180 to Caddo, then follow Park Road 33 north for 17 miles to the entrance. Look for whitetails along any of the park roads as well as along the shore of Possum Kingdom Reservoir.

Deer are plentiful in **South Llano River State Park,** too. Take U.S. Hwy 377 south from Junction for 5 miles, then turn on Park Road 73 for the short drive to the entrance. This park lies adjacent to the 2,123-acre **Walter Buck Wildlife Management Area,** where hiking trails and blinds can also be used to study the deer.

34

Salt Marshes and Tidal Pools

Quite possibly the most delicate habitats in Texas are the intermediate zones lying between the waters of the Gulf of Mexico and the firmer, higher ground of the oak mottes. Known as salt marshes, these wetlands support an amazing array of life forms ranging from microscopic plants to massive alligators.

Salt marshes don't surrender their secrets easily, simply because they're far more complicated than they first appear, but that's what makes them so much fun to explore. This month is a good time to discover the marshes because the warm weather helps make them more vibrant and alive.

Everything from the smooth cordgrass holding the sand and mud in place to the long-legged wading birds feeding in the shallow tidal pools to gather food for their recently hatched young occupies its own special niche in this unique environment.

The life blood of most salt marshes is the tidal pools, the small, shallow-water ponds that provide a starting point for not one but several food chains. The slightly greenish color of the water itself, for example, comes from the one-celled plants known as diatoms. These are eaten by various fish and insect larvae, which in turn are fed upon by slightly larger fish, which, in turn, are eaten by the birds.

The ponds are important for another reason. Many serve as nurseries for larger species of fish, such as the ocean-swimming channel bass or the redfish. Larger predator fish are largely absent from tidal pools, and the reedy, grassy shorelines provide hiding places from other predators. Food is abundant and includes not only the plankton but also the decaying vegetation, which help give a salt marsh its distinctive odor. Some fish, as well as a new supply of water, may come in daily on the high tides.

Many salt marshes also have freshwater pools, which are formed from rainfall. These are equally as important in the marshes, for they support entirely different food chains and help give the marsh its overall diversity. In some marshes, freshwater and saltwater actually mix, providing what is known as brackish water, and these have their own food chains.

Around the higher, drier dunes and grasses, snails, grasshoppers, crabs, mice, snakes, and alligators have their own niches. Because most salt marshes are fairly small, relatively speaking, it is easy to see how the various life forms are totally dependent upon each other and, thus, how fragile these ecosystems can be.

Even the vegetation has a role to play in this salt, sea, and land mix. The most abundant is the smooth cordgrass, one of the few rooted plants that grows well in saltwater, but there are bulrushes, salt grasses, shore grasses, even marsh elders in different places. Each pulls its own particular nutrient requirements from the ground and puts back something in return; it is a perfect example of biodiversity on a small scale.

While the vegetation is present at all times, in Texas the marshes and tidal pools are best known for their

Both the salt marsh tidal pools and freshwater ponds attract wading birds. In this small pond at Galveston Island State Park, egrets, spoonbills, great blue herons and white ibis share the water.

birds. They not only are the most visible creatures, they also exhibit the most diversity.

Flitting among the cattails and bulrushes will be red-winged blackbirds, seaside sparrows, and boat-tailed grackles. Around the edges of the tidal pools will be plovers, curlews, egrets, and great blue herons. The plovers and curlews will be probing their bills into the mud as they search for mollusks, crustaceans, and worms, while the egrets and herons will be stalking and spearing a meal of fish, frogs, and crayfish.

The open sand will be just as active. Fiddler crabs, easy to identify because one claw of the male becomes greatly enlarged during courtship, will be present. So will smaller ghost crabs, whose burrows in the sand are seen far more often than the crabs themselves.

In some salt marshes, the diamondback rattlesnake is a resident. Each September the female gives live birth to perhaps a dozen young snakes; eighteenth-century pirates in the Gulf called Galveston Island Snake Island because of all the rattlesnakes they found there. The snakes are still present, but they make as much effort to avoid humans as humans do to avoid them.

The salt marshes along the Texas coast had their beginnings several thousand years ago, as the ice from the last Ice Age melted and the level of the Gulf of Mexico rose. Sediments deposited by various rivers like the Trinity and the San Jacinto added to the sediment put down by the Gulf and formed the fragile but extremely fertile shoreline lowlands.

Galveston Island State Park

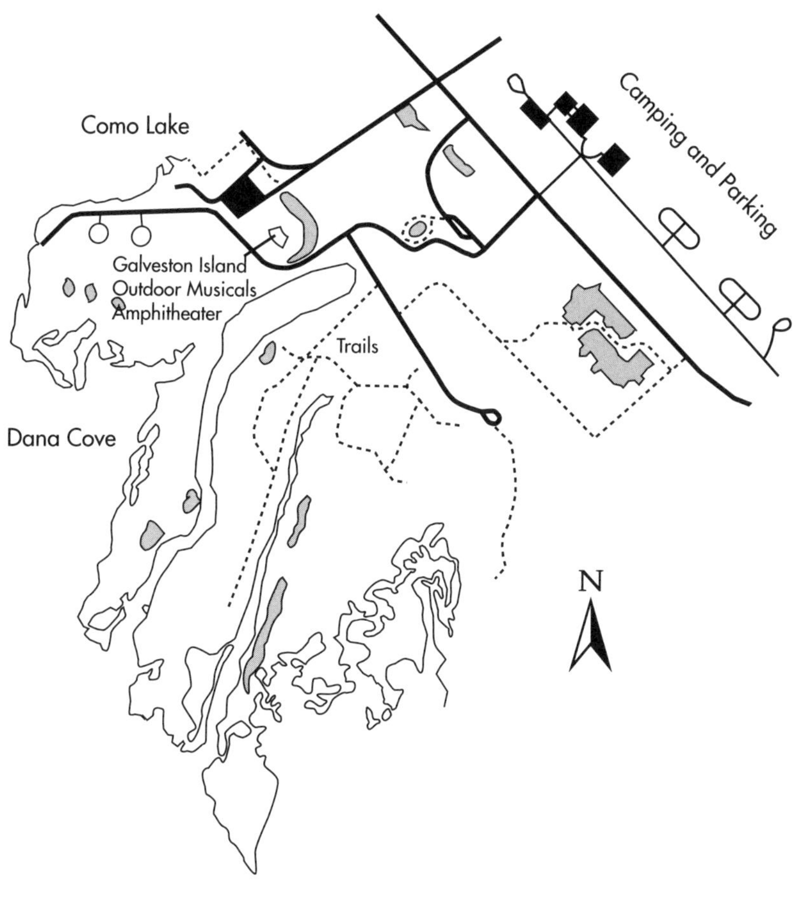

Hot Spots

One of the most interesting and accessible salt marshes, with its various tidal pools, is **Big Reef Nature Park,** located on the eastern tip of Galveston Island. To reach the park, follow Seawall Boulevard to the very end and turn right on Boddeker Drive. Follow this less than 1/2 mile and park across the road from Waddell's Bait Shop, on the left.

The park lies adjacent to Waddell's and includes a 2-mile guided trail through the salt marsh. More than 125 species of birds have been identified here, including the threatened piping plover. Peregrine falcons may also be present during the autumn.

Excellent examples of salt marsh and tidal pool habitat are also easily accessible at **Galveston Island State Park,** located on FM 3005 approximately 9 miles south of Galveston. The best marshes are on the north side of FM 3005, so turn right on Park Road 66 and then turn left at the Interpretive Trails sign. Walking trails lead into the marsh and beside tidal pools, where egrets, ducks, ibis, and other birds may be observed.

35

June Shorttakes

Mexican Eagles

Summer travelers in South Texas often see a large, dark-colored bird sitting on fence posts or perhaps walking quickly through the middle of a field as if searching for food. With long legs, dark wings and back, orangish yellow beak, white neck, and black head crest, the bird is hard to miss. It is the caracara, or Mexican eagle, so called because it is the national emblem of Mexico. Standing nearly two feet tall with a wingspan of perhaps four feet, the caracara is an aggressive member of the falcon family best known for its varied diet. One moment it will be scratching up grasshoppers and beetles from a meadow, the next it will be chasing vultures from a carcass. Snakes, fish, turtles, even baby alligators will be eaten if the opportunity arises.

The caracara is seen most frequently in **Kenedy, Brooks, Hogg,** and **Zapata Counties** and the **Rio Grande Valley Counties** to the south. Look for them along U.S. Hwy 77 between Kingsville and Harlingen; along U.S. Hwy 281 south of Alice; around the shore of Falcon Reservoir near Zapata; and in Laguna Atascosa National Wildlife Refuge near Harlingen.

36

A Closer Look: Nesting Sea Turtles

Among all the endangered species of wildlife throughout the world, one rather unheralded reptile has Texas biologists anxiously watching the beaches each summer. That species is the Kemp's ridley sea turtle, which in early 1996 was believed to number fewer than 400 individuals worldwide. The reason Texas has such strong interest is because the Padre Island National Seashore may have been an historic nesting area for the turtles. The island's biologists have been working since the late 1970s to restore them.

Ridleys, like all sea turtles, live all but a few hours of each year at sea. Those few hours on land are spent along remote beaches where they dig shallow nests in the sand and lay their eggs. Once that task is complete, the turtles laboriously make their way back to the water and essentially disappear for another 12 months.

The most famous nesting beach for the ridley has been just north of Tampico, Mexico, at a site named Rancho Nuevo, where tens of thousands formerly laid their eggs along just a few miles of sand. The ridley nested in denser concentrations than any other turtle, and it also came ashore during daylight hours, two factors that undoubtedly contributed to its heavy losses to predators, including human beings.

When ridley numbers had plummeted to just a few hundred by 1977, the Mexican government, the U.S. National Park Service, and other international agencies began what is known as the Kemp's Ridley Sea Turtle Restoration and Enhancement Project.

This project includes the transfer of ridley eggs from Mexico—where any type of natural disaster might wipe out the remainder of the species—to South Padre Island, where they are incubated, hatched, and released safely into the Gulf. Because sea turtles return to the site of their birth to lay their eggs, biologists hope the female ridleys will return to Padre after they mature in 10 to 12 years. So far, more than 18,000 eggs have successfully been hatched.

Four other species of sea turtle are occasional visitors to South Padre Island between April and September. These include the leatherback and the hawksbill, which are also listed as endangered, and the loggerhead and the green sea turtle, both of which are threatened.

Although nesting turtles are rare on South Padre Island, visitors do encounter the huge reptiles occasionally. Anyone who does is asked to carefully note the exact nest location and report it immediately to park officials.

Sea turtles have been on earth for nearly 100 million years and are believed to have changed very little in that time. Of the five major kinds of sea turtles, the leatherback, with its five- to six-foot soft shell is the largest; the ridley, with a hard shell measuring up to two feet in length, is the smallest.

The perilous journey of newly hatched turtles across the sand to the water has been well documented, but apparently all five kinds of sea turtles were able to maintain their historic populations against natural predators. Carefully controlled studies show a fascinating picture of how nature made it work. Each female turtle deposits just about 100 eggs each time she nests. Even though this is a small number of eggs when compared to other marine species, it does support the theory of safety in numbers. All the hatchlings have a role in digging out of their sand nest—the studies show most individuals cannot do it alone—and when traveling as a group to the water, they move straighter and faster than single turtles do. Thus, even though gulls, terns, coyotes, and other predators will invariably take their toll on the young turtles, at least some will make it to the water.

What happens to them after they do reach the water is still much of a mystery. Because it takes a decade or more for the females to mature and because they grow so large during that time, most tags are lost. Perhaps if the ridleys return to South Padre, some of the answers may be learned.

July

Notes

37

Panhandle Prairie Dogs

Although small in stature, the black-tailed prairie dog of the Texas plains has a notable presence in the history of the American West. Captain Meriwether Lewis of the famed Lewis and Clark expedition wrote of them with awe and wonder, and Francis Parkman described them at length in *The Oregon Trail,* noting that their towns stretched for miles across the open plains.

It was Lewis who is believed to have given these small rodents their name. At first he called them "barking squirrels," for they do look like squirrels without the bushy tails, and their most oft-uttered vocalization is a sharp, high-pitched bark. The bark won out over appearance, though, and Lewis settled on the name prairie dog.

There are two types of prairie dogs, the black-tailed and the white-tailed, although the latter has never been as numerous as the former, perhaps because it tends to inhabit higher altitudes (up to 10,000 feet) and harsher climates. The black-tailed prairie dog prefers the plains and even semidesert terrain and at one time almost certainly was one of the most numerous mammals in North America.

Since pioneer days, prairie dogs have captured the imagination of the American public, not so much because of their huge numbers but because of their personality. They're sociable among themselves, often hugging and even kissing one another. They're often observed romping, running, and wrestling playfully, and on warm summer evenings, adults and their young will sometimes gather near their burrow entrance and simply watch the setting sun.

Prairie dogs are gregarious little creatures, living in loosely organized "towns" that are actually divided into specific family or "coterie" territories. A coterie usually consists of one or possibly two males, several females, and their offspring. Other prairie dogs are not welcomed into another coterie's territory, although an intrusion seldom results in a true fight.

Individual prairie dog tunnels are far more complex than town organization; each burrow may extend as far as 80 to 100 feet underground. Although no two burrows are the same, most have similar characteristics. The tunnel slopes sharply downward for as much as 10 to 12 feet, then turns to one side and becomes a long corridor. Off this corridor are various rooms or chambers, seemingly with specific uses. At least one will be a nursery and another will be for refuse and waste. There is also a guard room close to the surface where inhabitants can listen or smell for possible danger before venturing back to the surface. When they are on the surface, at least one prairie dog will always be on sentry duty, and a single sharp, high-pitched bark will be enough to send the entire population scampering to their burrows for safety.

The tunnels provide homes for a wide variety of other plains wildlife, whether the prairie dogs are present or not. Snakes, rabbits, weasels, mice, toads, and even turtles use them. Insects find them particularly attrac-

Prairie dog colonies or "towns" once were scattered throughout Texas, but now their range is limited to scattered areas in the Panhandle where their daily antics provide hours of watching fun for visitors.

tive; in several burrows in Oklahoma one scientist found 39 species of beetles.

Prairie dogs are most active in the early morning and late afternoon hours during the summer, while in the winter they take advantage of warm sunshine whenever it occurs. They do not hibernate, nor do they store food in their burrows. Prairie dogs eat a variety of grasses, seeds, and insects. Often, they'll enjoy a meal by holding it in their front paws while sitting upright on their haunches the way a squirrel does.

The breeding season takes place in February and March. A litter of from two to as many as eight pups is born a month later, and after about six weeks of nursing, they are taken above ground for the first time in May and early June. July is a good month to see them because the young are active and playful and do not necessarily respect the coterie boundaries.

Prairie dog populations have diminished greatly during the past 80 years, primarily due to poisoning by ranchers with aid from various government agencies. It was long thought that the rodents ate grass that could have been used to feed cattle. The burrows also presented problems; horses would step in them and sometimes break a leg.

Today, the majority of prairie dog towns are located on protected lands, and they are but a fraction of their former size. Despite their dwindling number, however, the prairie dogs remain as playful and curious as ever and appear to be enjoying life to the fullest.

Hot Spots

Prairie dogs are easy to see at **Muleshoe National Wildlife Refuge** south of the city of **Muleshoe,** where several small prairie dog towns exist. Once you turn off Hwy 214 onto the gravel driveway leading to refuge headquarters (a large sign marks the turn), look for prairie dog towns on either side of the road. The easiest to see will be on the right-hand (north) side just before you reach the headquarters building.

Another place to see prairie dogs at Muleshoe is along the mile-long road leading to Lower Pauls Lake. Follow 214 approximately 2 miles north of the refuge entrance and turn right (west) at the entrance sign. The town will be on the left side about 1/2 mile down this gravel road.

Prairie dogs are also present at **Buffalo Lake National Wildlife Refuge** south of Umbarger. From Umbarger follow FM Road 168 three miles beyond the entrance to the refuge. The prairie dog town is on the left and is marked by a small traffic pullout and several signs in the meadow beyond.

A larger prairie dog town is located just .3 mile beyond this one on the same side of FM 168. It is not marked, so look for the mounds of the burrow entrances.

Prairie dogs are also easily viewed in **Mackenzie State Park** within the city of Lubbock. This day-use park is located in the northeast corner of the city at Avenue A (U.S. 87) and East Broadway. Follow the exit signs off I-27 or exit Parkway Drive or Municipal Drive off Loop 289.

38

Roadrunners

Imagine, if you will, a small but agile bird building a corral of cactus around a sleeping rattlesnake, then waking the snake by dropping another cactus on its head. The reptile, enraged at being so rudely awakened, strikes at the arrogant bird but misses, impaling itself on the cactus spines. Further enraged, it strikes again, with the same result. Eventually, the rattlesnake becomes so exhausted from repeatedly hitting the thorns that it gives up and becomes an easy meal for the bird.

Such are the legends surrounding the paisano, or roadrunner, of Texas and the Southwest. No feathered flyer, including the bald eagle, wild turkey, or bobwhite quail, has as many admirers or enjoys such celebrity status as this long-legged denizen of the brush.

In July the birds are quite active throughout all but the very hottest part of the day chasing insects. This is when grasshoppers are readily available, and the birds can be seen literally plucking them out of the air. They walk through the weeds and brush, causing the insects to fly—if they don't get the grasshoppers in flight, the roadrunners watch where they land and nab them then.

Roadrunners do eat rattlesnakes, too, although they limit their diet to small ones, and they don't surround the snake with cactus. Instead, they are quick enough

Roadrunners are found throughout much of Texas but are most common in the northern and western parts of the state. The birds adapt well to human encroachment and are often found in neighborhood backyards.

to dodge a strike by leaping into the air, then they dash in to grab the snake's head with their long bill. From that point on, the snake's future is limited, for the road-runner quickly scoots to the nearest rock where it proceeds to pound the rattler's head until the snake dies.

In addition to snakes and grasshoppers, roadrunners eat lizards, grubs, spiders, and mice, all of which they find by endless patrolling through the often arid and inhospitable mesquite and cactus brush. This is when many visitors first glimpse them, for birds are frequently found foraging along trails, roads, and rural highways. In fact, the roadrunner is believed to have been named for its habit of racing alongside horseless carriages and, later, automobiles, seemingly just for the fun of it. It's been clocked at a speedy 15 miles an hour!

Roadrunners are members of the cuckoo family, which includes 127 members worldwide. The birds are actually more structurally suited for ground movement, for they have not only a streamlined body but also long legs. While they prefer running to flying, however, the birds are certainly able to take wing.

Roadrunners have four toes on each foot (zygodactylous), with two pointing forward and two rearward. This is a characteristic common to only a few birds, including owls, woodpeckers, and parrots, but in the case of the roadrunner, it has also contributed to the bird's lore and legend. The Pueblo Indians of New Mexico, for instance, who revere the roadrunner as a symbol of strength, believe that the tracks of a road-runner placed in the sand around a burial site will confuse any evil forces that might try to stop the safe passage of the deceased spirit into afterlife. With two toes pointing forward and two backward, the evil forces can't tell which direction the spirit has taken.

Certainly one reason for the roadrunner's prominence in folklore is the bird's personality. Here is a creature of contrasts: a bird that prefers the ground to the air, that often shows more curiosity than fear, and that seems to truly enjoy human company—there are numerous instances of roadrunners becoming pets.

Few think of the roadrunner as a song bird, and while it certainly cannot compare to a warbler in carrying a tune, the paisano does have a very definite, distinct call, which males make in the spring. It is a somewhat coarse "coo-coo-coo-ooh-ooh-ooh" and may be mistaken for the call of the mourning dove. When a female is attracted, the pair nest either in trees or thickets, and two to perhaps six or eight eggs are laid in April or May. Both parents help in incubation as well as in raising the young, which hatch in less than three weeks.

In Texas, roadrunner habitat stretches roughly west of a line from Fort Worth southward all the way to Brownsville. The bird appears most at home in the drier regions, particularly in the canyons and brushy ridges of the Panhandle, but it may show up anywhere, including a rancher's barn, a school yard, or even a city neighborhood.

Location of Welder Wildlife Refuge

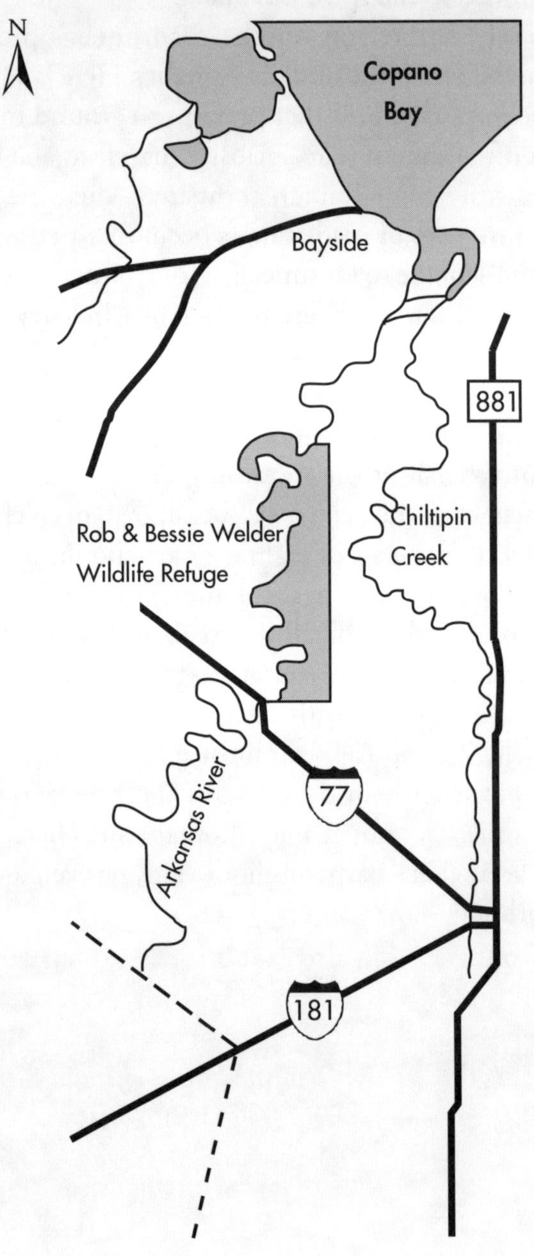

Hot Spots

Although roadrunners might be seen in practically any rural area in the western half of the state, one of the best places to view them is near **Caprock Canyons State Park** near Quitaque in Briscoe County. Look for the birds first along TX Hwy 86 west of Silverton, particularly after passing the turnoff for Ranch Road 145 when you're within 5 miles of Quitaque. Once in Quitaque, take Ranch Road 1066 north 3 miles into Caprock Canyons State Park. In the park, follow the main paved drive from park headquarters and look for roadrunners on either side of the road, especially between the Equestrian Camping Area and the Little Red Tent Camping Area. Roadrunners are also frequently spotted along the Eagle Point Hiking Trail (2 miles).

At the opposite end of the state, roadrunners are quite numerous in the **Welder Wildlife Refuge** located near Sinton in San Patricio County south of San Antonio. This private, 7,800-acre refuge is open to the public only on Thursday afternoons; free two-hour tours begin at the front gate promptly at 3 P.M. Roadrunners are easily viewed as they search for food along both sides of the paved tour road.

Tour goers can also expect to see whitetail deer, wild turkey, and dozens of species of birds at this refuge. Additional information is available by contacting the Welder Wildlife Foundation, P.O. Box 1400, Sinton, TX 78387, (512) 364-2643.

39

Tracks in the Sand

It has been written that the Apache chief Cochise and his warriors were such good woodsmen they could track a shadow over solid rocks, telling you which direction it traveled and how long ago. Although this is an exaggeration, the Apaches did enjoy a reputation as superb trackers and most men and women today can only hope to gain a fraction of their skills. Tracking a bird or animal is like reading a short story that may or may not have a surprise ending. Following the tracks is really the easy part; interpreting them and learning the story they tell is what makes tracking so much fun. As a tracker you don't have to sit and wait for nature to come to you because you can go to it.

Since Texas does not receive very much snow, the most consistent opportunities for tracking occur on sand, along beaches and the accompanying dunes. In the dunes, especially, you'll find a variety of life forms traveling to and fro that leave their prints behind. Other opportunities for tracking exist in practically any of the state parks around lakes and streams or wherever the ground is soft and moist after a rain.

In July, most wildlife will be active only on the edge of daylight, either very early in the morning or very late in the afternoon. In some places, much of the activity will occur at night. Regardless of when tracks are made, learning to follow and interpret them requires a little bit of detective work.

Before you begin, try to learn something about the animals and their habitats in the area you'll be in. Determine what species are most common, then study pictures of their tracks to help you identify them. Several excellent guidebooks are available for this, and many parks have printouts showing the tracks most often seen there.

In the Texas sand, a wide variety of creatures may leave their tracks for you to follow. Everything from small birds and lizards to larger predators like raccoons and skunks might be present. Whitetail deer, rabbits, and even coyotes are also species whose tracks you may encounter.

You can look for tracks practically anywhere the soil conditions are right, but some spots tend to be more productive than others. Some species, such as whitetail deer, coyotes, and even wild turkeys, often walk along unpaved roads. Others, like raccoons and herons, are frequently found near water, and still others may be more common around trees, brushlines, or the edges of meadows.

The first track you see is always the most exciting because it tells you you're in the right place, that something moved through this very same spot earlier. Now you get to follow the proverbial trail of crumbs to see where it leads.

Look at the track in the sun so it will appear sharper and deeper. As you begin to follow it, don't spend all your time looking straight down. Instead, scan the terrain ahead to see where the tracks may be leading or to possibly gain a better picture of what the animal may have been doing. Are the tracks in a fairly straight line or does the trail veer from side to side or go in circles? A straight line of tracks may indicate the creature was moving ahead to a specific destination, while a trail that circles and deviates indicates the animal spent time investigating or feeding. You may even see where the trail you're following intersects with the trail of another animal, or even more intriguing, where another creature begins following or stalking the same one you're following.

One goal of tracking, of course, is to find tracks with feet still in them—seeing the creature as it leaves its own footprints. This is not easy, but with practice you can accomplish it, and when you do, you'll have discovered a new way to enjoy the outdoors.

Hot Spots

Without doubt, one of the best places to try tracking is at **Monahans Sandhills State Park,** about an hour west of Midland off I-20 in Ward County. Here, 3,840 acres of sand dunes, some 70 feet high, are crisscrossed with the trails of desert residents. To reach the park, turn right on Park Road 41 at the entrance sign when traveling west on I-20 from Midland. Once in Monahans, stay on Park Road 41 to any of the parking pullouts, where you can start looking for tracks.

Galveston Island State Park offers sandy beaches and dunes that are also ideal for testing your tracking skills. From Galveston, follow FM 3005 approximately 10 miles west to the park entrance on the left. Park in the picnic or day-use area adjacent to the headquarters and start looking for tracks in the dunes behind the building.

40

Summer Spoonbills

While experienced ornithologists occasionally have difficulty identifying certain species, even the most inexperienced observer rarely misses when the subject is a roseate spoonbill. If nothing else, their name gives them away: rosy pink plumage and long, spoon-shaped bill. Without doubt, they are among the most popular birds along the Texas coast during the summer months.

The roseate spoonbills are the largest members of the ibis family found in North America, standing nearly three feet tall and having a wingspan of over four feet. Historically, their range has never been far from the Gulf Coast. While the birds will feed in saltwater, brackish water, or even freshwater, spoonbills show a definite preference for the coastal marshes and tidal flats between Texas and Florida.

It is here, where it can find mollusks, crustaceans, and small fish on the outgoing tides, that the bird shows the advantage of having such an unusual bill. In his *Life Histories of North American Marsh Birds,* Arthur Cleveland Bent quotes Audubon (1840) in describing how the birds secure their food:

> The spoonbills immerse their bills in the water or soft mud, sometimes with the head and even the whole neck beneath the surface. ... They move their partially opened

> mandibles laterally to and fro with a considerable degree of elegance, munching the fry, insects, or small shellfish, which they secure, before swallowing them.

The birds wade rapidly, swinging their opened bills through the water; nerve endings on the inside of the bill signal when to snap the jaws closed.

Audubon also describes seeing thousands of roseate spoonbills along the coast during his travels, but like the egrets, the spoonbill became a victim of its own beauty. Market hunters decimated spoonbill colonies to collect the plumes, but instead of selling them to adorn hats as the egret feathers were used, the spoonbill plumes were made into fans.

Fortunately, the bird rebounded well after the era of market hunting ended, and today it inhabits much of its historic range along the Gulf. It nests along the Texas coast on the man-made spoil islands in Galveston Bay, where eggs hatch in April and May. Not surprisingly, the baby chicks are born pink and with a spoonbill already formed.

Hot Spots

Without question, the **Bolivar Flats Shorebird Sanctuary** on the Bolivar Peninsula offers one of the finest birding opportunities in the United States, and this month roseate spoonbills will be on the flats along with many other species. The 5-mile north jetty, built in 1898 to protect the mouth of Galveston Bay, has produced the flats. It diverts currents that parallel the coast and causes sediment to fall out; in the nearly 100 years since the jetty was constructed, some 500 acres of flats and beach marsh have accumulated. The sanctuary, maintained by the Houston Audubon Society in cooperation with the U.S. Fish and Wildlife Service, embraces just over 1,000 acres and serves as a roosting, wintering, and nesting area for thousands of birds.

To reach the sanctuary, drive east on TX Hwy 87 approximately 4 miles from the Bolivar terminal of the Galveston-Bolivar ferry and turn right on Rettilon Road. Drive not quite 1 mile to the beach and turn right (if the sand is hard) on the rutted road to the sanctuary. Pilings, an observation tower, and a large sign mark the entrance. If the sand is soft, park at the end of Rettion Road and walk to the sanctuary.

Sea Rim State Park also offers the chance to see spoonbills, although better viewing opportunities here often require a canoe or quiet johnboat. The headquarters entrance is on the Gulf side of Hwy 87 and offers a long boardwalk through the marsh where the spoonbills occasionally feed. On the opposite side of Hwy 87 in the Marshland Unit, you can launch your boat and follow a network of water trails through the marshes.

Farther south, look for roseate spoonbills at **Goose Island State Park,** where they are also year-round visitors. To reach the park, follow TX Hwy 35 north from Rockport 12 miles, cross the Copano Bay causeway, and turn right on Park Road 13. South of the causeway in Fulton, look for spoonbills around Rattlesnake Point off FM 1781; this is a long point extending into Copano Bay and is a good place to spot additional shore-bird species.

You should also be able to spot roseate spoon-bills in the shallow waters of the Laguna Madre, the protected bay of the **Padre Island National Seashore.** To reach the Seashore, follow TX Hwy 358 east out of Corpus Christi; it will turn into Park Road 22. Follow Park Road 22 south for approximately 13 miles to the entrance.

41

July Shorttakes

Summer Star Gazing

Astronomers have been coming to the Davis Mountains in West Texas for more than 60 years to study the night. The higher altitudes and the low humidity—which mean clearer skies—aren't the only reason they've been attracted here to study the stars, either; the nights are actually blacker and produce a better contrast.

To take advantage of this unusual combination of features, the University of Texas constructed **McDonald Observatory** atop 6,800-foot Mount Locke north of Fort Davis. The original 82-inch telescope was completed in 1939; four others have since been added, including a 107-inch model that is the largest in the world. With these powerful telescopes, scientists have been able to study the heavens and provide critically needed information for NASA space probes.

McDonald Observatory has one of the most active public visitation programs of any observatory in the United States. To reach the observatory, follow TX Hwy 118 northwest from Fort Davis for 18 miles and turn right at the entrance sign. For additional information, contact the observatory at Box 1337, Fort Davis, TX 79734, (915) 426-3640.

42

A Closer Look: The Armored Armadillo

The armadillo may not be the largest mammal in Texas, but it undoubtedly ranks as one of the most interesting, and visitors from far and wide include the little armored creature on their must-see list before they leave. The animals are especially active in summer when they can be observed foraging throughout the day.

A member of the primitive order Endentata, the nine-banded armadillo of Texas is closely related to the anteaters and sloths of South America. Relatives include such bizarre cousins as the giant armadillo (five feet in length) and the fairy armadillo (five inches in length), as well as the hairy armadillo (its scales are covered with hair).

To some, the little 12-pound armadillo of Texas looks like a miniature dinosaur of sorts, due to its bony, plated, armorlike shell. These plates are arranged in nine joined but separate, flexible bands that give the animal its name. Additional scales cover the head, legs, and tail.

Most of the armadillo's life is spent shuffling noisily through the underbrush rooting under leaves and logs for insects, worms, grubs, and ants. With its keen sense of smell, some researchers believe the armadillo can smell these creatures as much as four or five inches underground.

By contrast, the armadillo's eyesight is considered very poor. That is why, when it hears or perhaps senses

Armadillos are found throughout Texas and are often seen along roadsides and in open meadows.

danger, it often stands upright on its hind legs to smell whatever might be threatening. When it does scent something, it makes a wild dash through the woods to a burrow, or perhaps to hide under a brushpile. Minutes later, when all seems safe, it will ease out to begin feeding once more.

Much of an armadillo's feeding is near water, and when an armadillo needs to cross a ditch or small stream, it does not hesitate to walk across—completely underwater—on the bottom. In deeper water or for longer crossings, the animal can inflate both its stomach and its intestines with air for buoyancy, after which it swims across.

Armadillos are also unusual in that the female always bears a litter of four young, all of the same sex. Research has shown that these are identical quadruplets, all formed from the same egg. Born in March or April, the young remain with their mother until the next breeding season. Their armored shell does not harden, however, until they are completely grown.

Although armadillos are eaten in both Central and South America, their value in the United States comes from medical research. Armadillos are the only known mammal besides humans that can be infected with leprosy, the chronic disease that deforms the skin. Researchers are using armadillos in hopes of finding a cure.

Today, after apparently crossing the Rio Grande into Texas from Mexico sometime in the 1870s or 1880s, the armadillo is widespread throughout the state. By the 1930s, in fact, the animal had spread into the Southeast. Because it is very susceptible to prolonged cold temperatures, however, its range limit has probably been established.

August

Notes

43

Late-summer Hummingbirds

Rare, indeed, is even the most casual wildlife watcher who has not been enthralled at least once by a hummingbird. These tiny acrobatic fliers, whose weight is measured in grams rather than ounces, are the smallest birds in the world but among its most popular.

Although more than 300 species have been identified, hummingbirds are found only in the New World and are most numerous in Central and South America. In the United States, 18 species have been observed, nine of them in Texas where several spend the summer.

Each is a unique marvel of nature's engineering. With wings beating as many as 75 times a second, they can zip along at 50 miles per hour. They can fly straight up, down, and sideways, as well as hover in place—but they cannot glide or soar.

Some species migrate more than 2,500 miles annually, including a nonstop flight across 500 miles of the Gulf of Mexico, but they do not walk or hop. They must consume at least half their body weight in sugar daily to maintain such an energy level, but each night hummingbirds go into virtual hibernation, their body temperature dropping to that of the surrounding air.

If it is not their aerial antics that enthrall observers, it is the brilliant iridescence of their colors. Reds, greens, purples, and even browns flash in the sun like signal mirrors, particularly in the males of the different species. This is due not only to the colors of each feather but also to their structure—they're practically like prisms in the way they reflect light.

Birders everywhere attract hummingbirds to their yards by planting various flowers like azalea, morning glory, hibiscus, and columbine, but most put up special feeders filled with sugar-and-water mixtures. Once the birds locate the feeders, they usually visit them several times an hour.

In Texas, most hummingbirds are either migrants or seasonal residents during the summer months. Birders usually hang their feeders in late spring and take them down in the fall after the birds have migrated to their wintering areas in Central and South America.

Hot Spots

Although hummingbirds can be seen throughout Texas during much of the summer and early autumn, it is difficult to actually see them in the wild. They may stay around certain flowering plants for a few days, then move to another area for a week before returning again.

One of the best places to see wild hummingbirds is in the **Demonstration Garden** in **Rockport.** Here a variety of flowering plants attract hummers, particularly in late summer and early autumn as the birds come into the region and increase their feeding to add fat reserves for migration across the Gulf.

The Demonstration Garden is in the city of Rockport on U.S. Hwy 35 North at the Texas State Department of Transportation picnic area. It's 3 to 4 miles south of the causeway bridge and on the left side of the road as you're traveling south. There is a pullout for parking as well as several picnic tables, walkways, benches, and a small freshwater pond. The Demonstration Garden was created, in fact, to attract hummingbirds and butterflies.

Each September the cities of Rockport and Fulton conduct the Hummer/Bird Festival, a four-day festival dedicated to informing the public about these tiny birds and timed to coincide with the fall migration of hummingbirds through the area. Speakers from throughout the United States give seminars on a variety of topics, including a demonstration of hummingbird banding. Several homes in the area also open their grounds to visitors to show how they attract the birds. For information, contact the Rockport-Fulton Area Chamber of Commerce, 404 Broadway, Rockport, TX 78382, (800) 242-0071.

44

Alligators

A little more than 200 years ago, while traveling through the South, famed naturalist William Bartram wrote in his journal, "The alligators were in such incredible numbers and so close together from shore to shore, that it would have been easy to have walked across on their heads, had the animals been harmless."

Today, the alligator is not quite as numerous as in Bartram's day, but for a creature that has been on earth for some 200 million years, it is still very visible especially during the warm days of July and August. And, not surprisingly, people remember alligators not because of their beauty but because of their ugliness; here is a huge reptile that looks not only prehistoric but menacing as well.

In truth, alligators do not present any real danger to people as long as they are not unduly disturbed. For the most part, they prefer to spend their time dozing in the sun or drifting quietly in a pond or lake as they search for food. They aren't even particularly aggressive hunters, generally feeding on whatever opportunity provides. Big alligators can actually go weeks without eating, if necessary.

While alligators do not pose much of a problem for people, people have been a major problem for alligators, and not because of habitat loss. As long ago as the

1850s, alligator hides became fashionable for shoes, luggage, and handbags, a fad that continues to this day. Within a century, alligators had very nearly been hunted and poached into extinction.

In 1970, the alligator was put on the endangered species list, and its comeback was so quick and successful that some states were allowing controlled hunts for them less than 15 years later. Today alligators thrive across the Gulf Coast from Texas to Florida and as far north as Arkansas and the Carolinas.

Alligators are closely related to crocodiles; there are 22 crocodilian species worldwide, although only two are true alligators. Generally speaking, alligators are fatter and more sluggish than crocodiles, and their snouts are broader and more blunt.

Surprisingly, the muscles that open an alligator's mouth are very weak and a man with average strength can hold an alligator's mouth closed with one hand. Even the largest alligators can quickly be put to sleep, too, if you can get one over on its back and start rubbing its stomach.

Alligators hatch from a clutch of eggs laid in the late spring. A female may lay as many as a hundred eggs, but the average number is usually less than half that. The eggs are covered with decaying vegetation and hatch in just over two months.

Scientists have discovered that the sex of alligators is determined by the amount of sunlight and heat each egg receives during incubation. Because increased heat produces only males, the female knows instinctively to move some of her eggs into the cooler, more protected parts of her nest.

In the wild, any alligator longer than 10 to 12 feet is considered quite large. Some may grow to nearly 20 feet in length, but most probably average less than 10 feet from the tip of the snout to the tip of the tail. A 12 footer, however, may weigh more than 400 pounds. Growth is about a foot per year until the reptiles are about six years old, when growth begins to slow. They are cold-blooded, however, and never actually stop growing.

In many areas, alligators perform valuable acts of conservation. They dig small ponds that trap water, and in times of drought these ponds help support many other forms of wildlife. Fish, turtles, birds, and insects all flock to these areas for survival.

Hot Spots

Brazos Bend State Park provides an excellent opportunity to see alligators at close range, and in fact, the park is filled with "alligator etiquette" warning signs. One of the best viewing spots is Forty-Acre Lake, which is reached via a short walk through the woods from the main park road. The trail leads completely around the lake and includes an observation tower. Signs mark the location of the trail.

Other viewing areas in the park include Pilant Slough, Elm Lake, and both Old and New Horseshoe Lakes, all located just off the main park road. Hiking and biking trails connect all of these lakes, and alligators are usually seen from the trails.

The park is located approximately 50 miles southwest of Houston near Needville. Travel south from Houston on TX Hwy 288 to Rosharon, then west on FM 1462 to the entrance. Information is available from the Superintendent, Brazos Bend State Park, 21901 FM 762, Needville, TX 77461, (409) 553-5101.

More than 200 alligators inhabit **Aransas National Wildlife Refuge,** but the easiest ones to see are those in Thomas Slough, directly across the entrance road from the visitor center and in Jones Lake reached by a short walk from the auto tour road.

Aransas NWR is located approximately 8 miles south of Austwell off FM 2040. Signs point the way. For information, contact the Refuge Manager, Aransas National Wildlife Refuge, P.O. Box 100, Austwell, TX 77950, (512) 286-3559.

Armand Bayou Nature Center just south of Houston also has some alligators, which are often

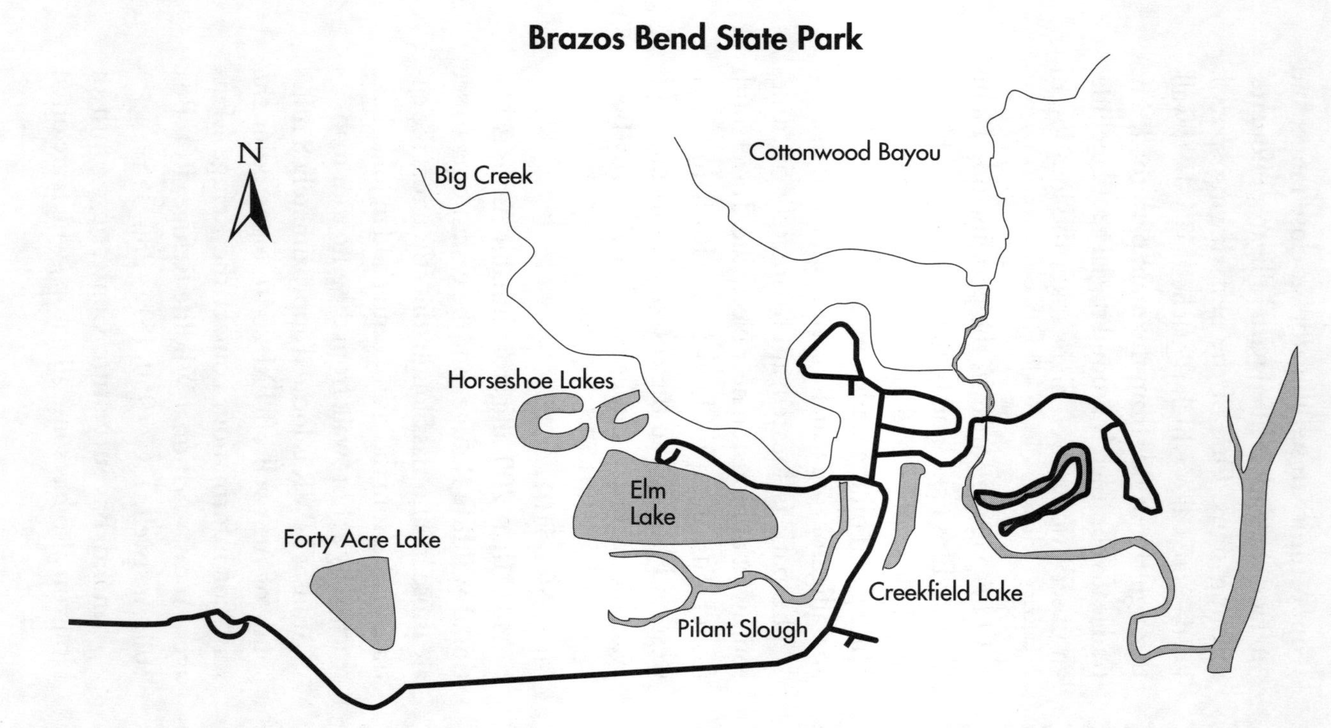
Brazos Bend State Park
N
Big Creek
Cottonwood Bayou
Horseshoe Lakes
Elm
Lake
Forty Acre Lake
Creekfield Lake
Pilant Slough

seen basking in the sun along the edge of the bayou. The center embraces approximately 2,500 acres and also has a large population of deer and birds. The hours of operation are 9 A.M. to 5 P.M., Wednesday through Saturday, and noon to dusk on Sunday.

To reach the center, follow I-45 south from Houston, then exit east on Bay Area Boulevard. Follow this 6.5 miles to the entrance. An entrance fee of $2.50 per adult is charged. For information, contact Armand Bayou Nature Center, P.O. Box 58828, Houston, TX 77258, (713) 474-2551.

45

Bat Watching for Beginners

If you have spent very many quiet summer evenings in the Texas Hill Country watching the sun set behind the far ridges, you have probably also seen one of nature's most efficient eating machines at work, although you may not have noticed. They begin appearing, alone or perhaps in small groups, just before dusk, and they'll stay aloft for most of the night, performing an endless array of swooping, darting, and diving maneuvers.

They are bats, and this is their nightly feeding ritual. Before dawn each of these flying acrobats will have caught and consumed hundreds of mosquitoes, moths, and other insects; a large colony of bats will consume several tons of insects nightly. These flying mammals—they are not birds or rodents—are easily some of humankind's best friends.

Nearly 1,000 species of bats are found throughout the world, 44 species in North America. Although most are insect eaters that save farmers and ranchers billions of dollars each year in crop damage, other bats eat fish and some even eat frogs. Still others, like the Mexican long-nosed bat, live on cactus nectar and act as pollinators, just like bees. They particularly like the agave plant, which is the basis of Mexico's tequila industry. These bats also help spread cactus by dispersing seeds

At dusk on most summer nights at several bat caves in the Texas Hill Country, millions of bats emerge to begin their nightly feeding. A colony of bats will consume several tons of insects each night.

in their droppings. Bat droppings, or guano, has had other uses, too. During the Civil War, bat guano from Texas caves served as a source of saltpeter, an important ingredient in gun powder, for Confederate forces.

Despite their huge economic importance, the bat's role in society has been defined by Bram Stoker's famous vampire, Count Dracula. Although there are vampire vats that do live on blood, it is from cattle, not humans, and they are not found in the United States. Other misconceptions about bats that have captured the imagination are that all bats have rabies and that they will readily attack people.

These misconceptions are beginning to get buried as more and more people learn of the economic benefits bats provide. In fact, many homeowners are constructing special bat houses around their yards to help control mosquitoes and other flying pests. Farmers and ranchers lucky enough to have bat-infested caves on their property are protecting them now rather than bulldozing them closed.

In the air, bats generally look much larger than they are. That's because of the swept-back wings that allow them to perform those loops and dives. Most bat bodies are only about the size of your thumb, and a bat's total weight is calculated in grams, not pounds.

The most amazing characteristic of the bat is its radar tracking system that allows it to locate flying insects. Not all radar tracking systems are the same for each species, either. One species, the California leaf-nosed bat, emits high-frequency signals through its nose and picks up the returning signals in its ears. Other bats use their extraordinary hearing to pinpoint prey—some can hear an insect walking on the ground—while others use equally keen eyesight to locate such foods as ants, beetles, crickets, centipedes, grasshoppers, and cockroaches.

Bats live in large colonies that frequently have several million members. Females normally give birth to a single pup each spring in a particular cave that acts as a nursery for the entire colony. The young are kept there for a month or longer until they are able to fly and feed on their own, at which time they move to a location that the colony uses as a daily resting area. This is why most bat colonies swell so dramatically in size during the late summer.

Throughout the summer, the bats perform their nightly aerial shows, but by early autumn many Texas bats begin migrating to their winter caves in Mexico. The following spring they return to the same roosting and nursery caves back in Texas.

Hot Spots

The Texas Hill Country, particularly the region between San Antonio and Austin and westward to Del Rio, is known as the bat capital of the United States. That's because 33 of the 44 species of North American bats can be seen in Texas, many of them in this region of limestone caves, warm temperatures, and abundant food.

America's true bat man, Merlin D. Tuttle, the founder of Bat Conservation International, which was formed to protect bats around the world, moved his headquarters to Austin because of the abundance of bats. Downtown Austin actually boasts one of the premier bat-viewing sites in the state, the **Congress Avenue Bridge** crossing Town Lake, where as many as two million bats emerge each evening between April and October.

To reach the bridge, exit on Riverside Drive from I-35. If you're driving south on I-35, you'll exit right on Riverside, left if you're driving north. Turn right at the third stoplight on Riverside, which will be Congress Avenue, and follow this to the public parking lot and large observation area. Bring your lawn chair or a blanket and plan to arrive at least 30 minutes before dusk.

Because the actual emergence time varies during the summer, contact Bat Conservation International (P.O. Box 162603, Austin, TX 78716, (512) 327-9721) for the latest information.

Another favorite viewing area is **Old Tunnel Wildlife Management Area** near Fredericksburg, where perhaps 2.5 million Mexican free-tail bats emerge from an old railroad tunnel. To reach the area, follow U.S. Hwy 290 east from

Fredericksburg for approximately 3 miles and turn right on Old San Antonio Road. Look for the sign pointing the way to Grapetown. Follow Old San Antonio Road for approximately 10 miles until you see the Old Tunnel Wildlife Management Area sign and gravel parking lot on the left.

Because of limited space and amphitheater seating—the bats emerge within a few feet of spectators—reservations are required at Old Tunnel. Tours are conducted each Saturday between June and October; the actual emergence can be as short as 10 minutes or as long as an hour. Additional information is available through Pedernales Falls State Park, Rt. 1, Box 450, Johnson City, TX 78636, (210) 868-7304.

Reservations are also required to watch the bats emerge at **Kickapoo Cavern State Park** north of Brackettville. To reach the park, follow FM 674 north for 20 miles to the entrance. Bat-viewing tours are conducted between April and October. For specific times and reservations, contact the park at P.O. Box 705, Brackettville, TX 78832, (210) 563-2342.

46

Red-cockaded Woodpeckers

Of all the members of the bird world, few appear as well adapted to their particular niche as the woodpeckers. It has taken millions of years for them to evolve, but how else do you explain a bird that acts like a feathered jackhammer as it drills hole after hole in the trunk of a favorite tree—and seems to totally enjoy the head-pounding experience?

The adaptations include a sharp beak that literally acts like a chisel and is connected to the skull by tissue rather than bone so it can absorb the drilling blows; four toes (rather than the normal three) on each foot to help grip; and stiff tail feathers that help balance the bird on vertical surfaces. As if these were not enough, some woodpeckers have tongues equipped with tiny spearlike barbs that help hold insects, and others have tongues coated with mucous produced by special salivary glands that helps collect ants. Most woodpeckers also possess extraordinary hearing, which they use in locating insects underneath the tree bark. All of these attributes help make woodpeckers extremely valuable to people, as their diet includes a wide menu of wood-boring insects that frequently damage not just individual trees but entire forests. In August, woodpeckers are often quite visible because the insects are most active in the warmer temperatures.

The woodpecker clan includes more than 200 species worldwide, but only 23 have been reported in the United States. In Texas, 14 species have been identified. Among them are several varieties of flickers and sapsuckers, including both the yellow-bellied sapsucker and the red-headed woodpecker, which are often seen in wooded backyards. The big pileated woodpecker, with its flashing red crest, black body, and laughing call, is a year-round resident in many areas.

Also present is the endangered red-cockaded woodpecker, which, according to a 1995 census, numbers less than 1,000 birds statewide. The red-cockaded woodpecker's low numbers are caused by its very specific habitat requirements and the loss of that habitat. It lives in mature, old-growth pines that have been standing for at least 60 to 70 years, and there aren't a lot of those left.

The majority of red-cockaded woodpeckers today live on government property, primarily national forests and designated wilderness areas, but in the summer of 1994, Champion International, a timber management and forest products corporation, began managing one of its 2,000-acre tracts in East Texas for the birds. International still harvests trees on the land but is leaving a mature stand of long-leaf pine specifically for the red-cockaded woodpecker.

These birds live in small groups of two or more birds, each cluster inhabiting its own territory. Of these groups, only one pair is actually a breeding pair, although all the birds take turns incubating the eggs. Young are born between April and June.

Experienced foresters and birders can easily identify the nesting and roosting trees of these woodpeckers because in addition to their actual nest cavity, red-cockaded woodpeckers drill several other holes around the tree; sap leaks from these "wells" and acts as a deterrent to snakes and other predators. Over time the streams of sap turn white and are easy to see.

The red-cockaded woodpecker actually has very little red in its coloration. It has black and white bars across its back and a black head but a distinctly white cheek that quickly separates it from the hairy and downy woodpeckers. The tiny cockade, those feathers on either side of the crown, are red in the male, which gives the bird its name. It's about as large as a cardinal.

Hot Spots

Perhaps the easiest place to see red-cockaded woodpeckers is in the **Sam Houston National Forest** north of Houston where the U.S. Forest Service has constructed a woodpecker interpretive site along the side of the road where the birds nest. To reach the site, follow I-59 north from Houston to Cleveland and exit left (west) on FM 2025. Follow FM 2025 12 miles; the interpretive site is marked by a large sign and a parking area just before reaching the FM 2666 intersection.

Red-cockaded woodpeckers are also easily viewed in the Sam Houston National Forest near New Waverly. From Houston, follow I-45 north to New Waverly and exit left (west) on FM 1375. Follow FM 1375 approximately 5 miles to the interpretive area on the right.

Other good places to see red-cockaded, as well as several other species, are in the **Angelina National Forest** southeast of Nacogdoches. At the Boykin Springs Recreation Area, located off TX Hwy 63 south of Zavalla, the birds are frequently observed along the entrance road. Just over a mile along this road look for a sign noting red-cockaded woodpecker habitat; it marks the beginning of a short walking trail where nesting and roosting trees may be identified.

The woodpeckers are also seen along the Sawmill Hiking Trail in this same recreation area. As you continue along the entrance road take the gravel road (Forest Service Road 326) that forks to the left. Follow this approximately 4/10 mile to the intersection with FS 327 on the left; the Sawmill Trail starts on the right and leads from there to the Boykin Springs Lake swimming area. It's an easy walk and even more enjoyable if you take the spur trail to Old Aldridge. This will take you along what is known as the Scenic Bend of the Nechez, where you'll pass through a magnificent forest of huge oaks, pines, and beech trees.

During the breeding season between late April and mid-June, red-cockaded woodpeckers can be observed throughout the day in their nesting areas, but don't stay in the area long, as the birds are easily upset by human intrusion. In summer, the woodpeckers are most reliably seen just at daybreak or just before dark as they leave and return to their nesting trees.

47

August Shorttakes

White-Faced Ibis

One of the most misidentified birds in Texas has to be the white-faced ibis, simply because it has practically no white on it. The primary coloration appears to be black, although it really is closer to a dark purple; the feathers have a certain sheen to them in the sunlight. The name comes from a small patch of white behind the eye and under the chin. The white-faced ibis is usually mistaken for the glossy ibis, which likewise is dark and has little white coloration. The glossy ibis is not common in Texas, however, while the white-faced ibis is a resident and breeds on the islands in Galveston Bay.

While the various rookery islands are accessible only by boat, a good place to see white-faced ibis this month is **Anahuac National Wildlife Refuge** east of Houston. The birds are easily viewed by car from the dike roads around the ponds since they usually prowl near the shoreline for food. To reach the refuge, follow I-10 east from Houston approximately 60 miles. Turn south on TX Hwy 61, and continue south when this turns into FM 562. Turn east on FM 1985 and follow signs to the refuge.

48

A Closer Look: Yucca

Its flowers, buds, and fruits can be eaten. Its roots can be ground and shredded to make soap. Its leaves can be used to make baskets, rope, sandals, or even thatch a roof. Surely, among all the plants that grow across Texas, few have such varied uses as the yucca.

They are like desert evergreens, lending a splash of green leaves and creamy white flowers to the brown summer landscapes of western Texas. In this arid terrain, they often dominate, for some species grow more than 20 feet tall. All are members of the lily family, which hardly seems possible, since the lily is small and dainty and some yucca weigh more than 50 pounds.

All the yucca plants are characterized by stiff, sharply pointed leaves that grow in clusters around the stem. The flowers grow atop the stem and in mature plants may include hundreds of individual blossoms that can form a cluster two feet tall.

Surprisingly, self-pollination rarely, if ever, occurs among these flowers. That's the job of the yucca moth, a small white insect that lays its eggs in open flowers and spreads pollen at the same time. The moth lays one egg per flower and visits not only dozens of flowers but dozens of yucca. The moth larvae begin their development inside the yucca, then spend the remainder of the year underground. They emerge a year later when the yucca blooms again and repeat the egg-laying fertilization process.

Among the varieties of yucca is the giant dagger yucca *(Yucca carnerosana),* so named because its strong, broad leaves are nearly as sharp as daggers. Each new growth of leaves and flowers takes place atop the stalk, which results in a huge, treelike trunk that may be a foot in diameter.

Through the centuries, yucca have been used in various ways by the Native Americans, Hispanics, and early Texans. Even today its fruits, leaves, and roots play an important role in the lifestyle of rural Mexicans living along the Rio Grande.

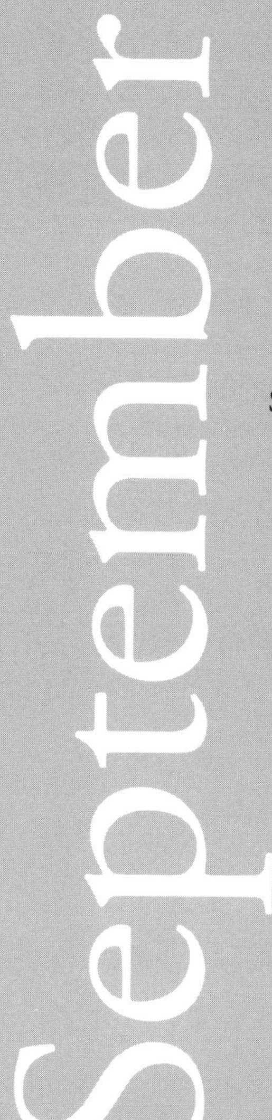

September

Notes

49

Desert Fir Trees

To trained and untrained observers of plant life, few plant phenomena are as mysterious as the presence in the modern world of "relic" species left over from ancient times. Such plants help scientists turn more pages in nature's book of world secrets.

Texas has several relic forests, perhaps the most dramatic being the Douglas fir trees growing in the Chihuahuan Desert of Guadalupe Mountains National Park. These trees are the descendants of fir trees that covered much of Texas 15,000 years ago.

The answer, not surprisingly, lies in a combination of geology and meteorology. Rock and weather conditions prevalent in the Guadalupes create the proper environment necessary not only for the Douglas fir, but also for the aspens and pines that grow with them, as well as a host of undesertlike wildlife that includes black bear and elk.

The Guadalupe Mountain range is the largest exposed fossil reef in the world, stretching some 400 miles from end to end. The peak of El Capitan, in the national park, marks one end of the exposed part of the reef. The steep, nearly sheer walls of El Capitan are characteristic of the abrupt elevation changes between the desert floor and the mountain summits throughout the range.

The suddenness of this elevation change is, to a large extent, why the fir trees have survived. The prevailing northwest winds are forced to rise when they hit the windward (western) side of the mountains. As the air rises and cools, clouds and rain form along the western slopes and over the summit, but when the winds and clouds sink again on the eastern slopes, they are dry.

That's why the eastern side of the Guadalupes is desert and portions of the higher slopes rich and green. The popular saying about some mountains "making their own weather" certainly applies to the Guadalupes; this park offers a unique look at several different life zones within an elevation change of a few thousand feet.

On the eastern desert floor the most common plants are yucca, agave, sotol, and cactus; hardy, unyielding plants that survive heat and wind with little water. Midway up the mountain slopes the plant life changes dramatically to piñon pine and juniper, and around 7,000 feet the Douglas fir survive in their own particular niche.

In Guadalupe Mountains National Park, visitors can hike to the summit of El Capitan, the highest peak in Texas, moving from a desert to alpine environment in just a short time.

Hot Spots

Within **Guadalupe Mountains National Park** the best place to observe and enjoy the cooling shade of the Douglas fir trees is in an area known as the Bowl, a 2-mile-wide depression reached by a somewhat strenuous 5-mile hike to an elevation of over 7,000 feet. The trail begins in the parking lot of the Pine Springs Campground, located off U.S. Hwy 62/80. Backcountry permits are required for overnight camping, and no water is available in the Bowl.

An easier hike to see the various ecological zones in the park is the McKittrick Canyon Trail, a 7-mile (round-trip) hike up McKittrick Canyon. To reach the trailhead, continue north on U.S. 62/80 toward Carlsbad, New Mexico, and turn left at the McKittrick Canyon junction sign. Follow this road approximately 4 miles to the visitor center and the trailhead. The trail begins in the desert only to change abruptly to a forest of oaks and maples—trees that shouldn't be here at all. This is a stunning hike when autumn color peaks.

50

Sandhill Cranes in the Panhandle

To the uninitiated, the flat, often featureless high plains of the Texas Panhandle may appear to be the most boring, least attractive terrain in the state. Trees are scarce, the wind nearly always blows, and the most common wildlife are cattle.

Starting in late September and continuing into February and March, however, this region changes its character dramatically, for then the plains become home to tens of thousands, sometimes hundreds of thousands, of lesser sandhill cranes. The highest number was recorded in 1981 when 250,000 cranes were counted at one site.

The number of cranes that stop here rather than continuing farther south to the Gulf Coast, or westward into New Mexico, depends, surprisingly, on water rather than food, for the sandhill crane is a land bird that requires water for nightly roosting.

In the Panhandle, this water is normally available in the form of thousands of small, shallow ponds known as playa lakes that are scattered across the region. In these shallow basins, where the water is often only a few inches deep, the cranes gather by the thousands each evening. They spend the hours of darkness standing shoulder to shoulder and foot to foot in the thin water, apparently feeling secure from any land-based predators like coyotes or bobcats. When there is little or no rain, these playa lakes dry up and the cranes go elsewhere.

The lesser sandhill is one of six subspecies of sandhill crane in North America and is by far the most numerous. The name "lesser" is almost a misnomer, for it certainly does not refer to the bird's size. Standing nearly four feet tall with a wingspan of six to seven feet, sandhill cranes are among the largest of all land birds.

They're basically gray-brown with a clearly visible red crown. Even more distinctive than this bright spot of color is the hoarse, croaking call the bird utters in flight. It has been described as prehistoric, trumpeting-like, and even "shaking the air," and it carries for miles; once heard, it is seldom forgotten.

Sandhill cranes nest in the high Arctic of Canada and Alaska, where a pair of chicks hatch in late spring or early summer. The birds leave the breeding grounds in August, rest and feed for a time in the prairie land of Saskatchewan, then continue southward to Texas. They depart in late February and gather by the thousands on Nebraska's Platte River for a rest stop before completing the northward migration.

The rich grainfields of the Panhandle suit the cranes well, for they are laden with the wasted grains of earlier wheat, corn, peanut, and milo harvests. From their roosting sites, the birds often fly 30 to 40 miles to find choice eating. They leave the roosts shortly after daybreak and enjoy a leisurely breakfast. The midday hours may be spent back at the roosting site, but more often they are spent in the air. Sandhills seem to enjoy gliding and spiraling ever upward on the rising thermals; they have been observed as high as 13,000 feet.

Each summer thousands of sandhill cranes arrive in the Texas Panhandle where they find a readily available food supply in the huge grain fields that are plentiful throughout the region.

By midafternoon the birds are back on the ground feeding again, and by early evening they have returned to their roosting lake. Although the cranes will use shallow streams and even farm ponds, they seem to prefer the larger playa lakes, where they crowd in side by side and often talk among themselves until well after darkness.

Muleshoe National Wildlife Refuge

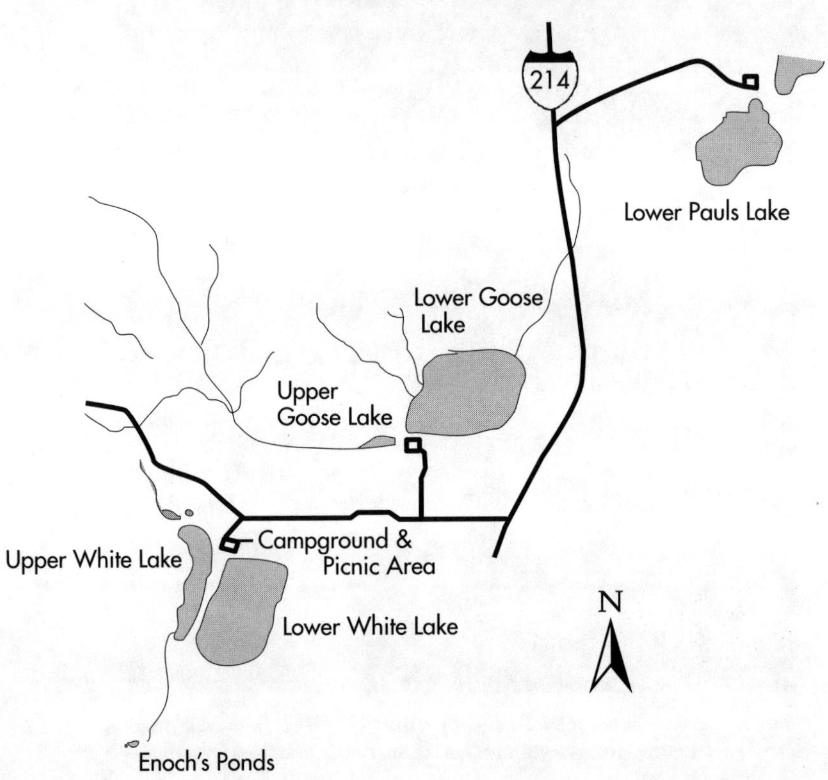

Hot Spots

Muleshoe National Wildlife Refuge, located approximately 20 miles south of Muleshoe on TX Hwy 214, includes three playa lakes that sandhill cranes use when water is available. Turn into the refuge off TX 214 and follow the gravel road leading toward the headquarters offices. Lower Goose Lake will be on your right, and Lower White Lake is farther down on the left. Both have parking pullouts for observation.

Lower Pauls Lake is a more reliable viewing spot, especially during a dry season. The entrance to this lake is also on TX 214, approximately 2 miles north of the main refuge entrance. Follow this gravel road 1 mile to the parking area.

Other places to view sandhill cranes are not as dependable, due to the changing availability of both food and water. The birds are often sighted northwest of the city of Big Spring near the community of Knott. Follow U.S. 87 north approximately 8 miles and turn west (left) on FM 846, then right (north) on FM 2230 in Knott. This leads through ranchland where the birds may be feeding.

Sandhill cranes may also be seen by turning right on FM 846 instead of left, then turning left (north) on FM 1584, a route that also leads through ranchland where several small playa lakes are located.

Up-to-date viewing information in this area is available by contacting the Big Spring Chamber of Commerce, P.O. Box 1391, Big Spring, TX 79721, (915) 263-7641.

51

Antelope Antics

In the world of nature, speed comes in many forms, but rarely does it appear as graceful, refined, and artistic as in the pronghorn antelopes. They are among the world's fastest animals, and when running, they have been described as phantoms floating on the wind. Top speed is every bit of 55 miles an hour, almost certainly higher for short bursts. Cruising speed is 30 to 35 mph, which they can keep up for miles. Even newborns can hit 20 mph within a few days.

The speed is simply part of the evolutionary process of survival, for pronghorns have been here for 20 million years. They are not true antelope but are the only remaining member of their own family of hoofed animals. They evolved totally in North America and have no close relatives anywhere else in the world.

The name "pronghorn" describes the distinct pronged horn found on the males. It consists of a hard, black outer sheath that covers an inner horn or core. Each fall this sheath is shed (but not the horn itself), and a new one is formed. No other animal in the world goes through this process.

Historically, pronghorns may have numbered as many as 50 million, ranging throughout the American West and Southwest, from Texas to California and as far north as Minnesota and the Canadian prairie provinces. They roamed the rough, arid, generally treeless plains and foothills side by side with the bison, and may have even outnumbered them.

Unfortunately, they could not outrun westward settlement, and by the early part of this century the pronghorn population had been decimated by uncontrolled hunting, fences, and loss of habitat. A 1924 census put their numbers at just 22,000, and it may have been considerably less. Today, through strong conservation efforts, the nation's total pronghorn population numbers around 500,000, and although its range is but a fraction of what it once was, the animal is doing well.

The first characteristic most people notice about these graceful little speedsters is their coloration. Rarely weighing more than 125 pounds or standing taller than three feet at the shoulder, they're a mixture of white and desert sandy brown, with perked-up ears, black eyes, and a decidedly white rump.

The white rump serves a special function among herd members, for it can warn of approaching danger. The muscles under an antelope's skin allow the animal to raise or lower its body hairs for added insulation or cooling, thus maintaining a constant body temperature. When the white rump hairs, which are nearly twice as long as the other body hairs, are raised, they also become a clearly visible signal to other pronghorns that it's time to run.

The second most noticeable feature about pronghorns is that they're nervous and fidgety, constantly looking about them as they browse across the rangeland. One of their defenses is their vision, which is extremely acute and allows them to see movement and potential danger from more than a mile away. When they do see it, they run. Individuals may suddenly stampede to a different clump of sage while eating, only to stop and walk back to their original spot; sleeping animals awaken with a startled jump and bolt across the plains for seemingly no reason at all.

It is behavior like this that makes antelope so much fun to watch, for at times they truly appear to be playing and enjoying it. Small groups will follow each other, alternately walking and running in single file for a mile or more across their rocky playground. At other times an entire herd will race a truck or automobile that happens to be moving through its range. Gradually their speed increases until without warning, but with uncanny timing, they dart right in front of the vehicle, only to stop and look back from a nearby vantage point as if waiting for applause and to emphasize their accomplishment.

Evolution has equipped pronghorns well for antics like this. The front feet are larger than the rear feet, to absorb the heavier pounding the front takes, and there is increased padding on all four hooves. The bones of the legs have tested stronger than those of a horse, and both the heart and the lungs are nearly double the size of those found in similar-sized animals.

The September rutting season usually provides additional antics. It often begins with one male trotting through the herd, pushing and nudging females into a separate group. Other males, of course, immediately begin doing the same thing, and because loyalties and respect aren't running too high at this point, they have no hesitation in trying to convince the ladies to join them instead. The first buck will run the intruder away,

Antelope are unusual in that they are uniquely North American, with no relatives anywhere in the world. They are easily seen in the ranch lands near the city of Marfa.

then wheel and race back to protect his harem, because undoubtedly another suitor will have appeared during the interim. By the time this one is chased away, the first intruder, or perhaps a third, is back. The confusion continues off and on for days.

Young are born the following May and June, and there are few indications the little four-pound bundles of fur will ever have the ability or the inclination to race a speeding car or train. Within a matter of only a few days, however, they'll be up to 20 miles an hour and from that point on they only get faster—and more fun to watch.

Hot Spots

Quite possibly the most reliable area of Texas in which to observe pronghorns is near the city of Marfa in Presidio County. Here the animals share open rangeland with cattle and are generally seen browsing near the highways. Follow TX Hwy 17 north from Marfa and begin looking for pronghorns on the left within two miles after leaving Marfa. Scattered bands live on both sides of the road for the next few miles. There is ample room on either side of the road to pull off for observation or photography.

Continue north from Marfa on TX Hwy 17 and turn left on TX Hwy 166 just south of Fort Davis to see additional animals. This road skirts the edge of the **Davis Mountains,** which rise abruptly out of the Chihuahuan Desert; antelope live in the gently rolling rangeland along the foot of the mountains. As the highway begins to gain altitude, you'll leave the antelope country behind; return to Fort Davis on TX Hwy 118, which cuts through the mountains, and then back to Marfa on TX Hwy 17. This 166/118 loop is known as the Davis Mountains Scenic Drive and is approximately 75 miles in length.

Antelope can also be seen south of Marfa for several miles along U.S. Hwy 67; as well as east and west of Marfa on I-90. In fact, antelope are present in various groups the entire 75 miles along I-90 west between Marfa and Van Horn.

Antelope are also easily viewed along U.S. 62/180 east of El Paso on the eastern slope of the Hueco Mountains. Follow U.S. 62/180 east for approximately 35 miles out of El Paso, then begin looking for antelope along either side of the highway once you pass through this small range of mountains.

52

Bugling Elk

Whenever hunters and wildlife photographers are asked to describe some of their most dramatic experiences, a common answer is often listening to a bull elk bugle on a crisp September dawn. It is an eerie sound that echoes down valleys and across meadows and through time itself; it is an ancient call that cannot fail to impress even the most seasoned wilderness lover.

Except for some animals in Guadalupe Mountains National Park, wild elk are not present in Texas, so the opportunity to hear one bugle is rare. Not far across the border into Oklahoma, however, at the Wichita Mountains National Wildlife Refuge near Lawton, a large elk herd has been prospering since the early part of this century.

The bugling is an integral part of the annual rutting, or breeding, but biologists do not honestly know why the big bulls make their eerie call. Shortly after rubbing their massive antlers free of velvet in August, the bulls begin gathering cows into harems. Collecting a dozen females is common, and the more dominant bulls may gather more than two dozen.

Throughout this gathering process—the rut lasts four to six weeks—the bulls also bugle. The call begins low and coarse but quickly climbs the scale into a strange, flutelike whistle, then drops again into a raspy cough.

At the peak of breeding activity, bulls may bugle every few minutes during the dawn and early morning hours, continue intermittently during the day, and begin again in the evening.

The call isn't to attract more cows, for the bull usually has a full-time job keeping the females he has from wandering away. It is not necessarily to challenge other bulls, either, because young and immature males will bugle just as often as an older monarch. It's as if the immature males are practicing for the mating wars that will follow in the years ahead.

Harem bulls are challenged regularly by other older bulls who want all or part of their harem, however, and this challenge may start by bugling. After meeting face to face, the two animals fight viciously with their antlers until one finally retreats. Rarely does death occur from these encounters, and normally they do not last very long.

Some biologists have speculated that the bugling is a form of advertising that serves primarily to alert other bulls in the vicinity, whether they have a harem or not. No two elk sound exactly the same, nor does the size or age of a bull have any real influence on how it sounds. Sometimes two bulls will bugle back and forth to each other without ever moving any closer; other times a single call will bring another charging in to fight.

After the rutting season, the bulls separate and frequently spend the spring and summer alone or in small groups while the cows gather in larger bands with their calves.

The elk that originally populated Texas and Oklahoma are believed to have been a subspecies known as the Merriam elk. The last Merriam was shot in Oklahoma in 1881, and the entire subspecies became extinct in 1906. The animals now surviving in the Wichita Mountains are Rocky Mountain elk and were brought to Oklahoma from the herd in Jackson Hole, Wyoming. Elk are the second largest members of the deer family, ranking only behind moose in size. Most believe they originated in Asia and gradually spread into different regions of the world where they developed into various species. They migrated into North America via the land bridge across the Bering Strait.

When the first American colonists arrived, elk were quite common from coast to coast except in the warm, humid Southeast. Because they are creatures of wilderness, the animals were quickly eliminated by the westward movement. Added to the loss of habitat was the problem that elk were prized for both their meat and their hides; by the late 1880s they had nearly been hunted to extinction.

Although the Wichita Mountains National Wildlife Refuge was established specifically for the protection of the bison that had shared their fate, a small band of elk was brought to the refuge in 1915. They found the rough, rocky mountainsides and rolling prairie land to their liking and have continued to do well ever since.

Hot Spots

The **Wichita Mountains National Wildlife Refuge** provides perhaps the best opportunity to see elk during the September-October bugling season. To reach the refuge, exit west onto OK Hwy 49 from I-44 just north of Lawton and follow this 7 miles to the refuge entrance. Follow the signs to the visitor center and headquarters for about 10 miles. Just beyond Osage Lake, you'll notice the high game fence on your right; start looking for elk anywhere for the next several miles.

One good viewing area is on the right less than a mile past the prairie dog town. Here a parking pullout offers long views of the rolling prairie that usually include several head of elk.

53

September Shorttakes

Aoudad Sheep

Aoudad, or Barbary sheep, are an exotic species of wildlife that were introduced into Texas in 1957. Natives of the harsh, rocky terrain of the Atlas Mountains in Morocco, they have not only survived but even thrived in the Lone Star State. Biologists estimate that there are now about 15,000 aoudads in the state, primarily in the Panhandle and Trans-Pecos regions.

Males and females have the same sandy brown coloration; thick, downward curving horns, and a beard of hair reaching from the throat to the forelegs. They are extremely wary animals, and, like most mountain sheep, are able to traverse steep terrain with ease.

September hikers may catch a glimpse of these unusual sheep in **Palo Duro Canyon State Park** near Canyon or in **Franklin Mountains State Park** in El Paso, although encounters will probably be brief, sudden, and surprising. A more reliable place to see them is at **Fossil Rim Wildlife Center** in Glen Rose, where a large herd is present and has become somewhat accustomed to human beings.

54

A Closer Look: Nature's Weather Forecasters

Rare, indeed, is the outdoors person who has not had an autumn outing ruined by an inaccurate weather forecast. People have been attempting to forecast weather since the dawn of civilization, but sometimes it seems the accuracy hasn't improved a bit! Ironically, nature has its own weather forecasters that often prove more accurate than all the satellites and radar available today. The two major indicators of future weather patterns are wind and clouds.

What is important about wind is not how strong it's blowing but rather the direction from which it is blowing and whether or not it changes direction. Generally speaking, wind that changes in a clockwise direction, such as from south to west to north (which it can do quickly) indicates fair or stable weather for at least the next 24 to 48 hours. When the wind shifts in a counterclockwise direction, such as from south to southeast, or east to northeast, look for a storm within the next 12 to 18 hours. This can be rain or snow, depending on the season of the year and the latitude in which you live.

Cloud formations are nearly as reliable as the wind in predicting weather conditions. Of all the formations meteorologists have divided cloud patterns into, the three most important are cumulus, nimbostratus, and cirrus.

Cirrus clouds are those high, wispy white streaks that usually include what are commonly called mare's tails. These fast-moving clouds (up to 200 miles an hour in some cases) indicate an approaching weather change, although not always one that includes precipitation. When these clouds appear, the next day will usually be cloudy or colder.

Nimbostratus clouds are the low, dark, thick clouds that eventually cover the entire sky. They forecast rain or snow. Cumulus clouds are the puffy white cotton balls that appear most often in summer. When they show up in the morning, it means there's a distinct possibility of rain by afternoon. Late-forming cumulus clouds are not nearly as accurate weather indicators.

Cloud direction and speed are also important to weather watchers. Clouds that move in a different direction from wind on the ground usually indicate warming temperatures ahead; clouds that race across the sky at high speed normally signal approaching rain.

Watching wildlife behavior can also provide a clue to what's ahead in the weather. Birds crowded on a power line, for instance, mean a storm is approaching. Why do the birds do this? The barometer is falling so the air is getting thinner and birds have more difficulty flying.

If you step outside to get your morning paper and there is no dew on the ground, start planning some indoor activities. Rain may follow within 12 to 24 hours. The dry ground may be followed with another accurate indicator of changing weather: a red sky at dawn. The well-known verse "Red sky at morning, sailor take warning; red sky at night, sailor's delight" describes two of the most accurate of all of nature's weather signals. They're even in the Bible in verses 2 and 3 of chapter 16 in the book of Matthew.

October

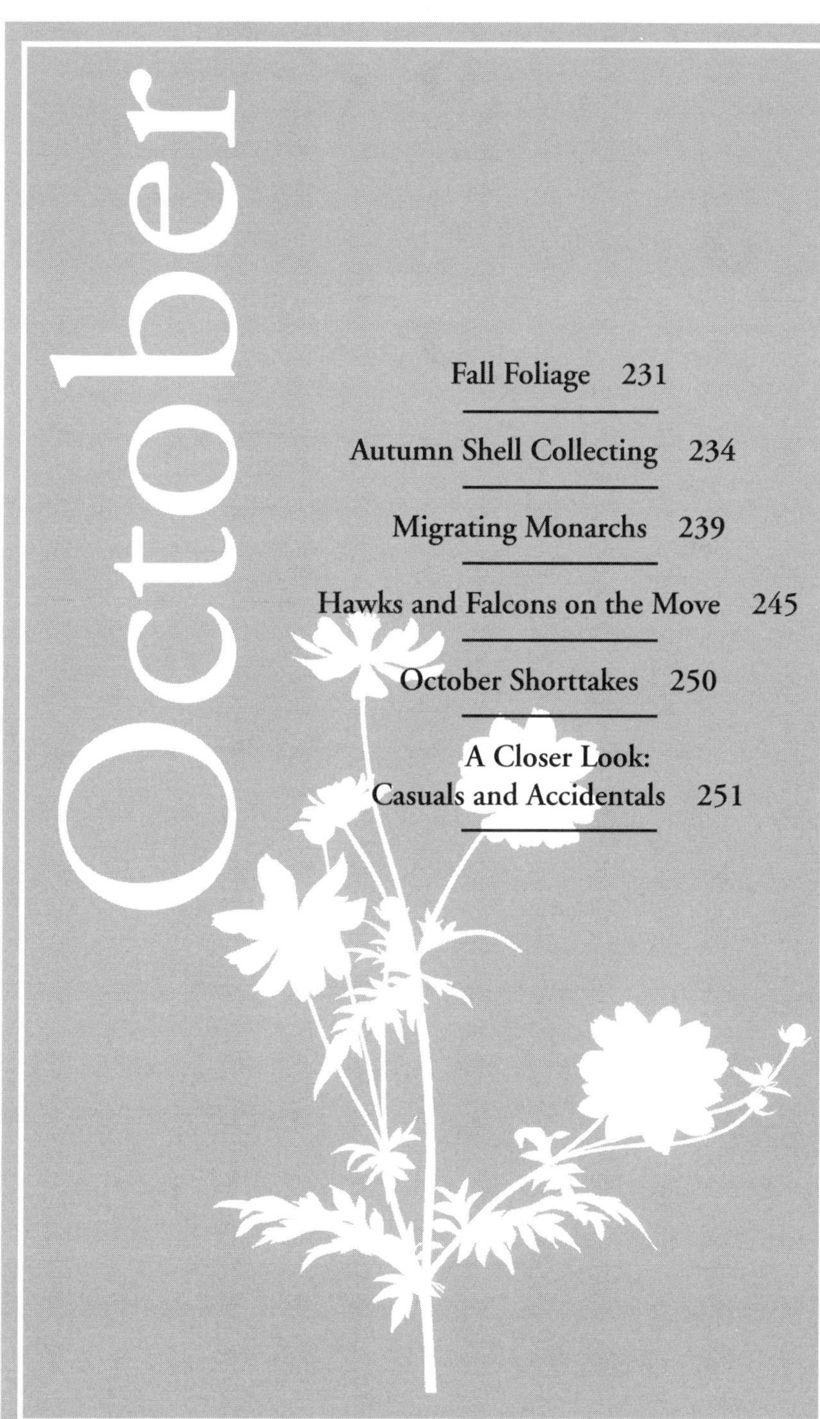

Notes

55

Fall Foliage

When the cooling winds of autumn carry geese southward, it isn't the only change they're bringing. One of the most visible changes occurs in the hardwood forests, where the leaves turn from summer green into a spectacular tapestry of reds, golds, oranges, and yellows. In Texas the change usually begins in mid- to late October and continues through mid-November, but some years the colors come early and other years later. Sometimes there is hardly any color display at all; no two autumns are the same.

Leaves change color because of the way sunlight interacts with their chemical pigments. The various pigments, such as carotene, which turns a leaf orange, or xanthophyll, which turns it yellow, are present in the leaves throughout the year, but the pigment that produces green, chlorophyll, is much more dominant. That is because chlorophyll is part of the process of photosynthesis, which takes place daily under the sunny skies of spring and summer. Chlorophyll breaks down quite easily, but under the bright sun a tree continues to produce and replace it.

As days become shorter and nights longer in the autumn, chlorophyll production slows, and gradually the leaf begins to die. As it does, the green coloration slowly gives way to other dominant colors of the species. Sycamores, for example, usually turn yellow, and cypress will turn gold. Maples and oaks often turn red.

If the autumn has been cool, clear, and dry for several weeks, leaf colors tend to be brighter and more intense, but a hard frost will kill leaves, causing them to fall with hardly a color change at all. A wet autumn may also knock leaves off trees before they completely change colors.

Hot Spots

Quite possibly the best-known spot for viewing fall foliage is **Lost Maples State Natural Area** in the Hill Country near Vanderpool. From Ingram, follow TX Hwy 39 west 27 miles to FM 187, then follow this south 14 miles to the park. The name derives from the relic forest of bigtooth maples that dates to the Ice Ages. Yellow, orange, and red are the dominant colors, and all are visible along the 1/4-mile Maple Interpretive Trail. An additional 10 miles of largely undeveloped hiking trails along the Sabinal River and its tributary creeks are lined with oak, ash, basswood, and other hardwoods that provide a dazzling array of autumn color.

In East Texas, **Martin Dies Jr. State Park** offers a chance to see cypress turn gold, followed by beech, sweet gum, and oak. The park is located just off U.S. 190 west of Jasper on the shore of B.A. Steinhagen Lake. Take the auto loop through the Walnut Ridge Unit (less than 5 miles total) on the north side of U.S. Hwy 190. If you're on foot, take the hiking trail around Gum Slough in the Hen House Ridge Unit on the south side of U.S. Hwy 190.

In far West Texas, the favorite fall color viewing spot is McKittrick Canyon in **Guadalupe Mountains National Park.** The 7-mile round-trip trail leads beside McKittrick Creek and into a steep-walled canyon where maple, walnut, and a variety of other hardwoods turn the desert a brilliant red, orange, and gold.

56

Autumn Shell Collecting

Among the millions of residents of Texas, there is a small group that hopes for hurricanes each summer, can't wait for a severe winter freeze, and eagerly looks for a flood. No, they're not weather forecasters, although many would probably like to be. Instead, they are shell collectors who prowl the state's hundreds of miles of beaches and bay shorelines searching for the tide-washed treasures in the sand.

The hurricanes, freezes, and floods always create better shelling opportunities because the mollusks—the soft-bodied animals living in the shells—are extremely sensitive to water and weather changes. Late-summer hurricanes tear them loose from the sand and other structures and wash them ashore, while prolonged cold temperatures or a drastic change in water salinity kills them outright. The animals can withstand brief changes by retreating into their shells, but they are not strong enough to survive more than a few days.

Another reason the colder months generally provide better shell collecting is because some Gulf currents actually change direction at that time. They don't change drastically but vary just enough to dislodge mollusks that may have otherwise escaped the force of the water. Shells like Scotch bonnets, the eastern murex, and others are washed ashore in the fall after being absent during the warmer spring and summer.

All of which makes the autumn and winter months

an excellent time to prowl the beaches looking for shells. In addition, at this time of year the crowds have departed, so the beaches are quieter and less disturbed.

The shells that show up on the coast are from mollusks, a huge group of invertebrate soft-bodied animals dating back more than 500 million years. The shells are their external skeletons. There are seven classes of mollusks comprising thousands of species, and in Texas the two classes most often found are bivalves and gastropods.

The bivalves include those animals whose shells have two halves, such as clams and oysters. On the beaches, however, only one half of the shell is normally found; the other half, originally attached by only thin muscle and tissue, has been ripped loose and could be miles away.

To the casual observer, it often looks as if no two bivalve shells are alike, for the designs and colors encountered seem endless. This variation is simply one way mollusks respond to changing conditions. Generally, however, enough basic characteristics remain so the shell can still be identified correctly.

The other mollusks most common along Texas shores are the gastropods, which are the snails. Along the beach they are represented by everyone's favorite shells, the whelks and the conches. The Texas coast does not produce large, pinkish conches like those on some Florida beaches but does provide any beach walker a wide and colorful assortment from which to choose.

The techniques of shell collecting are simple. All that's needed is a small bucket or collecting bag in which to put the shells. No permits are required by the state, and very little oceanfront property is off-limits. The best collecting time is at low tide when more of the beach and flats are exposed.

Casual collectors generally choose their "keepers" by color alone and limit their searches to informal strolls of short duration along convenient beaches where they happen to be visiting. Serious collectors not only visually inspect the sand but frequently dig in it as well. No piece of driftwood, seaweed, or other debris goes unsearched for a possible clinging shell.

Shell collecting has fascinated humankind in varying degrees for hundreds of years. Over time, shells have been used as money and trade barter, eating and cooking utensils, and, of course, decorations. Today, shell collecting is also a major business for some, as witnessed by the myriad of shells for sale in many beachfront shops.

Hot Spots

Mustang Island State Park has long been a favorite for autumn shell collectors because of its position as one of the state's barrier islands and because it receives less visitor traffic than the more famous Padre Island National Seashore to the south. To reach the park, take South Padre Island Drive (TX Hwy 358) out of Corpus Christi across the causeway bridge to Padre Island, then turn north on TX Hwy 361 (formerly Park Road 53) for approximately 22 miles to park headquarters. This highway continues north along the beach to Port Aransas; good shelling is available all along the route.

If you turn south off TX Hwy 358, the road becomes Park Road 22 and leads to **Padre Island National Seashore.** Here the two favorite areas are Little Shell and Big Shell beaches, named, appropriately enough, for the average size of the shells found on each.

Little Shell Beach begins south of Malaquite Beach at mile marker five; Big Shell begins at mile marker 20. At Big Shell, several Gulf currents converge just offshore and strike the beach at three different angles. Included here is a particular current known as the Devil's Elbow, which flows the opposite direction of the main Gulf current. The result is a larger than average selection of shells.

Matagorda Island State Park, north of Mustang Island State Park, has also been a favorite shelling area for years, due to the fact that the beach is never raked and therefore shells are not broken, and also because it receives much less visitor traffic. Accessible only by boat, Matagorda is reached by taking the ferry from Port O'Connor. The ferry offices and dock are located just off TX Hwy 185 at the Inland Waterway; signs point to the ferry office. Departures are at 9 A.M., Thursday and Friday, returning at 5 P.M.; and 8 A.M. and 10 A.M., Saturday and Sunday, returning at 3 P.M. and 5 P.M. year-round. The cost is $10 for adults, $5 for children.

Each winter, the Texas Parks and Wildlife Department offers several day-long shell-collecting trips to Matagorda. State park transportation takes visitors to the shelling area from the ferry landing.

57

Migrating Monarchs

Each autumn as ducks and geese begin their annual migrations south, another migration of the same type is already underway. It is one of the strangest occurrences in the natural world, for it is made by monarch butterflies. From their summer breeding grounds as far north as Canada, these tiny insects may fly 3,000 miles to wintering grounds in the pine and fir forests west of Mexico City.

Of the more than 17,000 different butterflies in the world, only a handful are migratory, and the monarch is the only one in North America. How the monarchs make such an arduous journey is only part of the riddle; how they find the wintering grounds is just as intriguing, since no butterfly makes the trip more than once.

The monarchs migrate in huge swarms rather than in small groups or individually. Those making the trip have emerged only a short time earlier from the pupal stage, but tagging studies have shown that they fly 80 miles a day during the journey, and in unusual cases, if they catch the right winds, the monarchs may cover several hundred miles in a day.

The migration begins in September, with monarchs in the central and eastern United States heading southwestward; it is estimated that more than 100 million reach Texas during the month of October. Two major flyways have been identified: one along the coast from the Louisiana border to Houston and then to Brownsville, and the other through the west-central part of the state from Wichita Falls to Abilene to Eagle Pass.

About a dozen roosting areas have been identified in the mountains west of Mexico City, all above 10,000 feet in altitude. In Texas, scientists and volunteer helpers tag thousands of monarchs each autumn in hopes of learning some of the answers to the questions surrounding this phenomenon. The west-central Texas migration route, for example, was confirmed by volunteer observers in 1994.

The migration must be seen to be believed. Dr. William Calvert of the Texas Parks and Wildlife Department describes one day during the 1994 fall migration in his newsletter, *The Texas Monarch Watch* (vol. 1, no. 2): "Over Kerrville around noon on October 9th, Monarchs poured through at a rate as great as 300/minute. ... We estimate that Monarchs may have traveled as far as 500 miles the day of October 9th when high velocity north winds were blowing over the state."

Monarchs return through Texas during a spring migration in mid- to late March, but it is more difficult to follow because not nearly as many of the butterflies return. Many of those that do, lay eggs soon after arriving in Texas. Within a month or so, these become butterflies and continue the migration northward. They breed several more times during the summer, and it is the generation born in early fall that makes the migration back through Texas to Mexico.

Monarchs and other butterflies, along with the moths, are members of the order Lepidoptera, which means "covered with scales." Tiny interlocking scales cover every part of the body except the butterfly's eyes, and are one reason the insect appears so colorful. They help reflect light just like a prism.

There are four stages in the life of most butterflies: egg, caterpillar (larva), chrysalis (pupa), and adult butterfly. The entire process of hatching from egg into caterpillar, producing a chrysalis, and metamorphosing into a butterfly can take as little as a few weeks to as long as several months. In one species, eggs develop directly into butterflies.

When butterflies emerge from the chrysalis, they are full grown, and although they drink the nectar from different flowers, they do not grow anymore during their lives. Some, in fact, survive only a few days; others like the monarch live for months.

The migration habits of monarchs are just part of the fascinating evolution of these insects. Butterflies are attracted to flowers by both sight and smell—the antennae on their heads can detect scents in the air—and while nectar is sucked in through a hollow tongue, butterflies also have taste organs on their feet. Just as unusual, butterflies require air to breathe, but they do not have lungs; air enters through tiny holes around the body.

Butterflies are cold-blooded, so naturally they are most active during the warmest hours of the day. Most are quite territorial, but they don't limit themselves to defending a particularly rich corner of a garden. They've been known to defend a patch of sunlight and even move as the sunlight moves!

Monarchs are the best-known butterflies in North America because of their brilliant orange coloration as well as their huge, cloudlike migrations. They're also well known in other parts of the world, including Canada, Australia, the West Indies, and South America.

Much of the monarch's spread geographically can be linked quite accurately to the spread of milkweed, the monarch caterpillar's primary food. In Texas, several different varieties of milkweed are popular garden plants, and all attract monarchs.

The Migration of Monarch Butterflies Through Texas

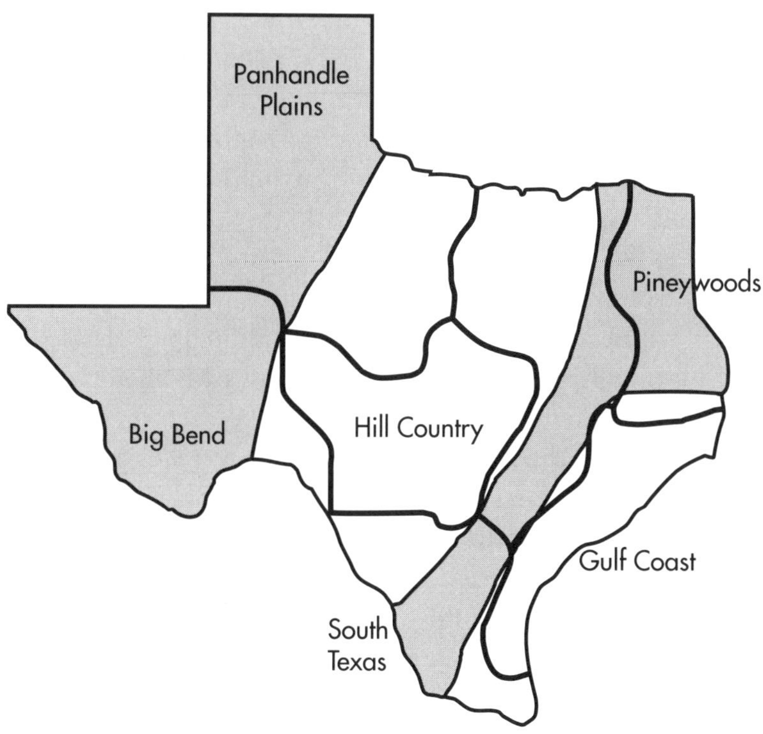

Hot Spots

One of the easiest places to view migrating monarchs is at **Mercer Arboretum and Botanical Gardens** in Houston, where much of the park's 214 acres includes flower gardens that attract many different species of butterflies, not just monarchs. Butterfly tagging is also performed by the staff. To reach Mercer Arboretum, exit east off I-45 to FM 1960. Follow this 3 miles and turn left on Aldine-Westfield Road and follow the signs. Hours of operation are 8 A.M. to 7 P.M., Monday through Saturday; 10 A.M. to 7 P.M., Sunday.

Another place where migrating monarchs are often seen is in **Seminole Canyon State Park** near Comstock. To reach the park, drive west on U.S. Hwy 90 from Comstock for 9 miles, then turn south (left) at the entrance sign.

Because the west-central migration flyway is approximately 200 miles wide, there are many other places where monarchs might be seen. One is around the city of Uvalde, particularly along U.S. Hwy 90 westward from Uvalde to Brackettville. Other cities to consider are Batesville, Carrizo Springs, Corpus Christi, and Austin. The Monarch Hotline, (800) 468-9719, provides up-to-date information on the migrations.

Volunteers interested in participating in monarch research and tagging can contact Dr. William Calvert, Texas Monarch Watch, Texas Parks and Wildlife, 4200 Smith School Road, Austin, TX 78744, (512) 441-0387.

58

Hawks and Falcons on the Move

Everyone has seen them at some time, either soaring lazily over meadows and fields or perched motionless high in trees or on telephone lines from which they appear to be surveying their domains. They have fascinated humankind for more than 4,000 years, but even today they are among the most misunderstood birds in the world. They are the hawks and falcons, which are most visible during their April-May and October-November migrations across the state. During these migrations, it is occasionally possible to see thousands of hawks in a single day.

The hawk family, Accipitridae, includes not only the hawks but also eagles, vultures, and kites, a total of 25 North American species, nearly all of which may be seen in Texas. The closely related falcon family, Falconidae, has just eight species found in North America, six of which may be seen in the state.

Of these two families, perhaps the red-tailed hawk and the peregrine falcon are the best known to casual birders. Many hawks are named because of some prominent color feature, and the red-tail is no exception. Its reddish brown tail provides quick identification when seen from either above or below. Pairs of red-tails are often observed soaring near each other high above brushy fields calling their high "keeeeer, keeeer" call to each other.

Other hawks often seen in Texas are the red-shouldered, broad-winged, Swainson's, white-tailed, Harris, and sparrow hawk. All are known as broadwings, because of the broad, rounded wings that allow them to soar in effortless fashion while hunting for mice, rabbits, and squirrels.

A few members of the hawk family, primarily the kites, have shorter wings and longer tails, which give them greater maneuverability so they can feed primarily on other birds. Included in this group are the Cooper's hawk, goshawk, and Mississippi kite.

Far less common and only occasionally seen is the peregrine falcon. It is well known, however, because of its comeback from the ravages of DDT insecticide as well as for its role in the ancient sport of falconry. Hardly larger than a crow, the peregrine's long, pointed wings allow it to reach speeds of nearly 200 miles per hour as it dives on its prey.

Even more rare is the aplomado falcon, which has been re-introduced into South Texas with chicks raised in human-made nests. In 1995 the first aplomado falcon in many years was born in the wild near Brownsville.

Although falcons and hawks are closely related, their nesting habits are entirely different. Most hawk nests are large and quite conspicuous; some may measure two to three feet across. Falcons, in contrast, don't build nests. Instead, they scrape a depression in mosses and gravel on steep rocky bluffs in which to lay their eggs, and they frequently return to the same spot year after year.

Migrations bring peregrines from Greenland and Canada across the central part of the United States each

Migrations of birds of prey are spectacular in South Texas.

spring and autumn to the Texas coast, where they stop for several weeks to feed and store body fat in order to continue their migrations. It is the only known staging area along their entire route, and it concentrates hundreds of birds in the state each April and October.

Due to their relatively large size, hawks must rely on convection currents, or thermals, during their migrations in order to save energy. Because these thermals do not form over water, the birds follow shorelines, and the configuration of the Texas coast funnels them through South Texas during their north and south migrations.

Many hawks migrate only as far as Texas from their more northerly nesting ranges; others, like Swainson's and the broad-winged, continue into Mexico and South America for the winter. The migrations are spectacular because of the sheer numbers of birds that might be seen in a day and are often well publicized in area papers.

Hot Spots

For many, **Kleberg County** ranks as the premier hawk-watching area in the state, and, indeed, the north-south strip of land between U.S. Hwy 281 and U.S. Hwy 77 between Kingsville and Harlingen-McAllen is often referred to as "hawk alley." Kleberg County, site of the famous King Ranch, lies partially within this corridor and to the east of Kingsville.

One particular hotspot is along TX Hwy 285, which crosses and parallels Los Olmos Creek. Take U.S. Hwy 77 south from Kingsville for 11 miles to Riviera, and turn west on 285. Follow 285 for approximately 22 miles to Falfurrias, where it intersects U.S. 281. You can make a loop trip here by turning north in Falfurrias on U.S. 281 and traveling about 20 miles to the intersection with TX Hwy 141, which leads east back to Kingsville.

Another favorite viewing area, especially for Mississippi kites and Swainson's hawks, is along County Road 2340 east out of Riviera. Follow this road several miles to FM 2510, where you turn right to reach the shore of Baffin Bay. Locally, this is known as Site 55, or the Texas A&I University Biological Station.

The **King Ranch** itself offers three-hour bird and wildlife viewing tours in which as many as 35 to 50 different species can be observed, several of which are usually red-tail and Harris hawks, along with the crested caracara. Reservations must be made through the King Ranch Visitor Center, located on TX Hwy 141 West in Kingsville.

Peregrine falcons frequently rest and hunt among the dunes of the **Padre Island National**

Seashore, but the birds have many miles of seashore to use, so getting to view them is never a sure thing. To reach the National Seashore, take TX Hwy 358 out of Corpus Christi and turn south on Park Road 22. Drive as far as you can, then plan to walk, either early in the morning or late in the afternoon. Many peregrines are observed on the western (Laguna Madre) side of the island, which means several miles of trudging through brush and loose sand, but others are seen on the Gulf side, where they perch on driftwood and other debris.

Laguna Atascosa National Wildlife Refuge near Harlingen offers excellent viewing possibilities for a variety of hawks. To reach the refuge, follow FM 106 east from the city and follow the signs.

59

October Shorttakes

Driving the River Road

Autumn ranks as one of the best times to visit the Chihuahuan Desert of southwest Texas because the weather is both cooler and wetter. Everything, from wildlife to plantlife, is more active. One way to get a feel for this desert environment is by driving **El Camino del Rio**, the River Road, just west of Big Bend National Park. Officially, this is FM 170, and the 50-mile route between Lajitas and Presidio is considered one of the most spectacular in the entire Southwest, as the road climbs and dips in and out of rugged canyons along the Rio Grande.

The volcanic action that shaped this part of the state is certainly noticeable, but the road also crosses several small creeks and skirts green oases where hawks, wrens, and other birdlife may be seen. Look for wildlife near Fresno Creek, Panther Creek, and Tapado Canyon.

The road is filled with sharp curves, steep climbs, and long descents; allow at least two hours for the trip. The best way to make this trip is by combining it with a visit to the national park or to the Big Bend Ranch State Park, which borders the road for most of its length.

60

A Closer Look: Casuals and Accidentals

Among ornithologists, few events create as much interest or excitement as the appearance of "casuals" or "accidentals." These are broad terms to describe birds that suddenly appear in an area where they normally are not seen. A casual visitor usually means one that has been reported in a state before but less than a dozen or so times. An accidental denotes a rarer appearance of a bird far from its normal seasonal range. In his book, *Birds of Texas,* Roger Tory Peterson defines an accidental as a species recorded five times or less in the state.

Birds become casual and accidental through a variety of causes. The most common reason is that they get blown off their migration routes in October and November because of strong winds or storms. Considering the small size of most birds, the distance they fly over water, and the intensity of both fall and winter storms, it's probably a miracle more don't end up lost.

Sometimes weary fliers take refuge on ships and ride off course, and a few probably overshoot their destination. Some scientists also believe that occasionally a bird's natural navigation senses become confused or inoperative, for whatever reason.

In Texas, accidentals and casuals are seen most frequently along the coast, since it is the first landfall for any birds migrating northward over the Gulf. Other key locales are the Guadalupe Mountains in West Texas, which collect mountain species from the western United States; and the pine woods of East Texas along the Trinity River, which can catch vagrants from anywhere in the eastern half of the United States.

The species that become casuals and accidentals in Texas do not fall into specific categories, although various warblers and hummingbirds are commonly reported. Over the years, the list has included everything from Arctic loons to flamingoes to great black-backed gulls.

News of the sighting of any casual or accidental travels fast among birders, some of whom may travel hundreds of miles for a brief glimpse of a new species. Such was the case during February 1995, when a pair of Mexican masked ducks were positively identified at Brazos Bend State Park west of Houston. Birds like this normally do not remain in an area for long, so viewing opportunities are usually limited.

The appearance of casuals and accidentals is important to biologists and other scientists for a number of reasons. Because birds are a barometer of environmental conditions, the unexpected arrival of a newcomer (and particularly several of the same species simultaneously) may indicate a new habitat search, such as that exhibited several years ago by the brown pelican along the East Coast. The bird now nests in states where before it was practically unknown.

If a bird is rare or endangered, any positive sighting may help shed light on the means to ensure its survival. This, in fact, is an annual quest of birders along the western end of Galveston Island who scan the grassy fields looking for an Eskimo curlew.

The Eskimo curlew may be extinct today; if it isn't, it's close. It nests in Arctic tundra, migrates down the Atlantic seaboard to Argentina for the winter, then returns to the Arctic by way of Panama and Texas. Hunted nearly to extinction a century ago, no birds were identified between 1905 and 1945. Then, two were seen on Galveston Island, and scattered reports have come periodically ever since. The problem is that inexperienced birders (and even experienced ones) may easily confuse the Eskimo curlew with the whimbrel, a similar bird and much more common.

Naturally, anytime a possible Eskimo curlew or any other unusual species is seen, the rare-bird telephone hotlines get busy. Because Texas is such an intense birding state, there are several such telephone numbers across the state (see below).

In addition, the Texas Ornithological Society monitors and evaluates casual, accidental, and especially rare bird sightings and encourages viewers to submit written and photographic documentation whenever an unusual species is observed. The information will be reviewed by the society's Bird Records Committee and added to the overall ornithological data in Texas. The society's address is 326 Live Oak, Ingram, TX 78025.

Rare-bird hotline telephone numbers include:

South Texas coast:	(512) 364-3634
Upper Texas coast:	(713) 992-2757
Austin area:	(512) 483-0952
North Texas area:	(817) 261-6792
San Antonio area:	(512) 773-8306

November

Notes

61

Rutting Whitetails

Among biologists, hunters, photographers, and wildlife watchers the story is often told of a whitetail deer experiment in Michigan's Cusino Wildlife Experiment Station in which six hunters were allowed to hunt 39 deer in a 1-mile-square, high-fenced block of forest. Of the 39 deer, nine were antlered bucks, and four full days elapsed before anyone saw them.

The story illustrates the personality of the whitetail deer, which seems to change dramatically after its antlers harden in September. During the summer the bucks are neither aggressive nor particularly wary; in November the bucks are preoccupied with two things, hunters and breeding does.

The breeding cycle begins when the bucks stake out private territories by "rubbing" the bark off small saplings and pawing the ground to create "scrapes" where they leave their scent. A doe, coming into heat for approximately 30 hours each 28 days until bred, leaves her own scent in the scrape; when the buck revisits the scrape, he detects her and begins trailing. For the buck, this entire sequence of events is known as the rut.

During this time, bucks also invade the territories of other bucks and fights occasionally take place, particularly in regions where does are not plentiful. The animals push, shove, and smack their antlers together until a victor is established.

Antler "rattling" to imitate the sounds of two bucks fighting, is a popular hunting technique throughout much of Texas, and it's a good trick for wildlife watchers and photographers to employ because it frequently brings bucks in at a gallop, apparently to steal the doe being fought over.

What is interesting about the rut is that it is often quite visible to observers, as this is when the bucks actually appear to lose some of their caution and spend more time in the open. They chase does, and once breeding begins may remain with that doe for hours, often standing beside her as she lies down to rest.

The onset of the rut is not uniform across the state. In some areas it begins in late November, while in South Texas it normally starts in mid-December. It is often said that cold weather triggers onset of the rut, but that is not completely true. A sudden plunge in temperature simply tends to make the animals more visible during the daylight hours because all deer are naturally more active in cooler weather. Otherwise, much of the rutting activity takes place at night.

Opinions vary on the precise origin of the whitetail, although many believe today's animal is the result of some 15 million years of evolution from various hoofed stock in Europe and Asia. Sometime in the dim past, deer were among those creatures crossing the Bering Strait on the ice. They continued to migrate southward until today they can be found all the way into Central America. Surprising, perhaps, is the fact that there are almost certainly more whitetail deer in North America today than when the colonists arrived. Much of the credit for the population growth must go to the

In autumn after shedding the velvet on their antlers, whitetail deer go into breeding season, or rut, which lasts for several weeks in November and December.

Texas has more whitetail deer than any other state, and the animals provide many hours of pleasure for millions of people.

whitetail's ability to adapt to a changing world. It can survive in extremely small areas in swamps, forests, fields, and even city suburbs. It is a creature of cover, and when food is available in that cover, the animal does not venture into the open often, except during the rutting season.

Hot Spots

Although whitetail deer are common in many state parks in the central part of the state known as the Hill Country, perhaps the best place to view them is in **Choke Canyon State Park** near the town of Three Rivers, south of San Antonio. This is the region known as the Brush Country.

Follow TX Hwy 72 west from Three Rivers for 11 miles to the entrance to the Calliham Unit of the park. A sign marks the entrance. Turn right on Ranch Road 8 and follow this 1 1/2 miles to the entrance. Just beyond the entrance, turn right at the stop sign pointing to the tent camping and shelter area. You'll usually see deer, as well as possibly wild turkey and javelina, at various places along this main road.

Deer can be seen here throughout the day because they are accustomed to traffic and campers. While it is permissible to leave a vehicle and walk through the mesquite, park officials discourage getting close to whitetails during the fall rutting season.

For other locations, see chapter 33, "Summer Whitetails" in June.

Choke Canyon State Park

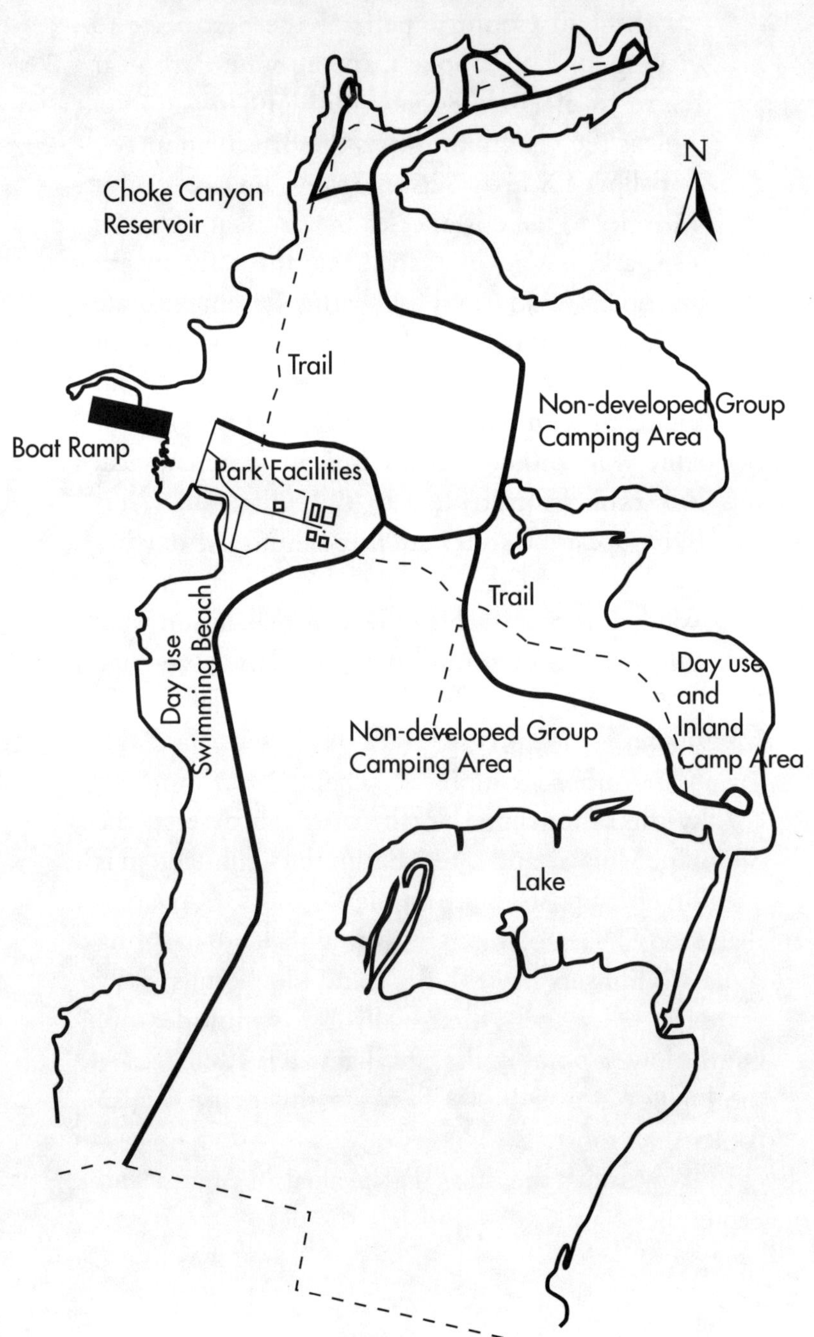

62

Desert Solitudes

If you spread a map of Texas before you and follow the path of the Pecos River from where it enters the state about 60 miles east of Guadalupe Mountains National Park southeastward to Amistad Reservoir on the Mexican border, you will have defined the eastern edge of one of the most unusual regions in all of North America, the Chihuahuan Desert. At 196,000 square miles, it is the largest of North America's four deserts, embracing all of Texas west of the Pecos, a sizable part of New Mexico, and an even larger portion of Mexico.

Included in this vast region are Big Bend National Park, Big Bend Ranch State Park, and Guadalupe Mountains National Park, three of the most fascinating and remote areas of Texas.

Like the other three North American deserts, the Sonoran, Mojave, and Great Basin, the Chihuahuan is a region of contrasts, but here the contrasts seem larger than ever. The region receives little rainfall, but in spring some wildflowers like the Big Bend bluebonnet grow three feet tall. Deserts are usually low in altitude, too, but the lowest point in the Chihuahuan is 1,800 feet—the highest is over 9,000 feet—so this desert is also cooler than most.

By November the rains that peaked in August and September have ended and left the desert green and cool. This, then, is an ideal time to walk the trails and prowl some of the rocky canyons. Chances are you'll have the land to yourself.

Much of the Chihuahuan is actually rolling grasslands, interspaced with isolated, independent mountain ranges. Hundreds of different types of grasses have been identified here, but a lot of the grassland has been replaced by shrubs like yucca and cactus. In fact, some 250 different species of cactus have been identified in the Chihuahuan Desert, more than in any other North American desert.

Besides the cactus, one interesting plant to look for throughout the desert is the lechuguilla *(Agave lechuguilla),* which, like all agaves, grows for many years before finally blooming. Some estimate the lechuguilla takes 30 years or more before finally flowering; a stalk suddenly grows 5 to 10 feet tall out of the cluster of spiny leaves, blooms for several weeks, then dies. During World War II the leaves were a source of cortisone, and for centuries Native Americans of the Southwest made rope and baskets from them.

The Havard agave *(Agave havardiana),* also found throughout much of the Chihuahuan Desert, takes even longer to bloom. Sometimes a half a century passes before flowering occurs, which is why it is better known as the century plant. Once the blooming process begins, it goes quickly; the flowering stalk may grow more than a foot in 24 hours.

Another oddity of the Chihuahuan Desert is the candelilla plant *(Euphorbia antisyphilitica),* which has been used for more than a century for the production of wax. When boiled in water, the plants release a natural wax that rises to the surface; it is easily removed and sold to processors throughout the United States who manufacture candles, waxes, and polishes.

Any autumn stroll should be planned to lead to one of the many springs that dot the Chihuahuan Desert. Small or large, each waterhole forms a desert wetland that usually produces its own tiny ecosystem. Here you'll find insects and perhaps small reptiles living and birds and mammals coming to drink.

The first thing you'll probably see is the small, green, spotted Rio Grande leopard frog, and if you don't see it, you'll likely hear it, since it seems to have a wide vocabulary of grunts, chucks, and growls. Its equally noisy cousin, the canyon treefrog, lives around water at higher elevations.

Somewhere in your desert sojourn you may also encounter one of the ferocious looking but totally harmless tarantulas. They've been on earth pretty much as you see them for millions of years, and while they will bite in self defense, their bite is not poisonous. In fact, these spiders make good pets and will actually learn to recognize their owners.

The truth of the matter is that if you're looking for solitude in the Chihuahuan Desert, it may be hard to find if you watch the ground, the plants, and the air around you. The desert is alive day and night with one of the most fascinating arrays of plant and animal life found anywhere in the world.

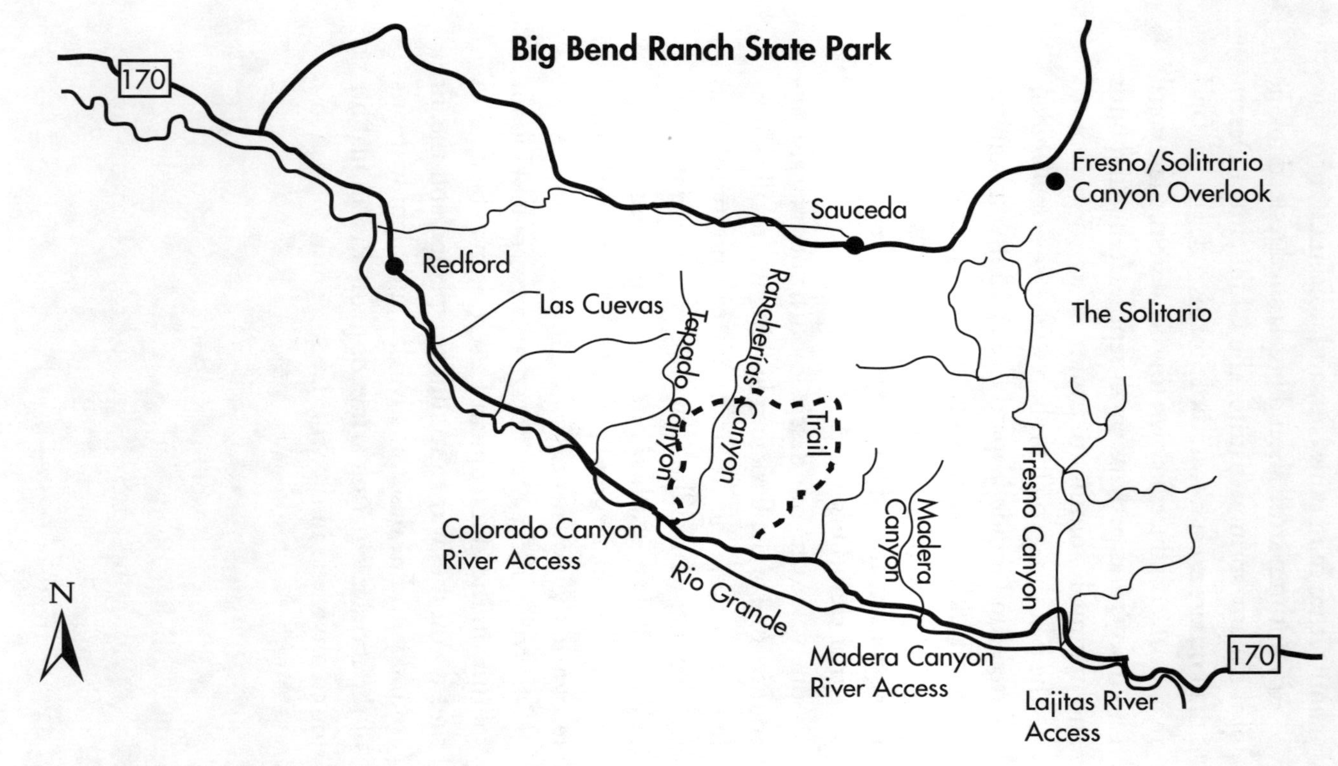
Big Bend Ranch State Park
170
Fresno/Solitrario
Canyon Overlook
Sauceda
Redford
Las Cuevas
Tapado Canyon
Rancherías Canyon
Trail
The Solitario
Madera Canyon
Fresno Canyon
Colorado Canyon
River Access
Rio Grande
Madera Canyon
River Access
170
Lajitas River
Access
N

Hot Spots

One of the best places to sample the Chihuahuan Desert in its purest form is **Big Bend Ranch State Park,** which is generally described as a living library of natural history. Several trails are open for hiking and backpacking.

The shortest and easiest of these is the Closed Canyon Trail, a 1/2-mile path along the floor of a narrow, erosion-cut canyon. Water is present, so you'll see that part of the desert ecosystem. To reach the trailhead, follow FM 170 west from Lajitas about a mile beyond the East Rancherias trailhead and look for the parking lot and sign.

Another longer trail, the 4-mile (8 miles round-trip) Rancherias Canyon Trail, follows the canyon floor to Rancherias Falls, an 80-foot waterfall. Along the way you'll pass several seasonal springs that show the importance of moisture in the desert and the variety of life it supports. The trailhead here begins at the same point as the West Rancherias trailhead, which is about a mile beyond the Closed Canyon Trail. The West Rancherias Trail is a 19-mile loop that takes about three days to complete.

Another way to see Big Bend Ranch State Park is by guided bus tour. Trips depart at various times from the Warnock Education Center in Lajitas or from Fort Leaton State Historic Site, located just south of Presidio on FM 170. Reservations are required, and a fee is charged.

Numerous walking opportunities also exist in both Big Bend National Park (See chapter 22, "Blooming Cactus" in April) and Guadalupe Mountains National Park (See chapter 49, "Desert Fir Trees" in September).

63

State Champion Trees

Rare, indeed, are the opportunities to walk in the shaded understory of ancient hardwood trees, experience "darkness at high noon," and listen to owls hoot in the middle of the day. Even more rare is the person who is not moved by such an experience.

Often it is described as a feeling of awe, of wonderment, and of reverence. Mountains, as majestic as they may be, do not impart the same feelings. Nor do deserts or rivers or grasslands, even though each is older than any living tree.

Giant trees leave us humble because they are living, breathing organisms like us. They have survived storms, fires, insects, and harvesting, to say nothing of beating the odds against simply taking root in the beginning. Only in the old forests are we able to feel our own beginnings.

In most instances in the southern forests, age also means size. The older the tree, the larger it becomes, until it may be 150 feet tall and 15 feet in circumference. We are awed because they are so rare; today's trees are largely part of second- and even third-growth forests that were originally cut at the turn of the century. Hardwoods like magnolia, ash, and cherry were taken for furniture, boxes, and baseball bats.

The southern forests are especially fascinating because they include such a vast mixture of species. Over the past several million years, as each succeeding Ice Age pushed glaciers southward, different species of trees retreated ahead of them. Then as the ice melted, the trees progressed northward. This is why it is possible to see northern species like the various hickories and American beech growing close to pines, magnolias, and cypress. These wonderfully mixed forests, still in huge blocks and essentially untouched for centuries, are what greeted the loggers of 1900.

Although the majority of the big trees were cut, here and there some escaped the saw and ax, and later the bulldozer and skidder. Today, the largest survivor of each species is designated as a state champion or even a national champion tree, and most are found in protected forests or wilderness areas where logging and clearcutting is now prohibited. November is one of the better months to view them because the weather is cooler and the insects usually less aggressive.

In Texas, 10 state and 3 national champion trees are found in the national forests located just over an hour's drive from Houston. In the Angelina, Davy Crockett, and Sabine National Forests, it seems totally out of place to find a bald cypress 500 years old, a loblolly pine more than 150 feet tall, and a grove of black walnut trees, but they're there.

Few are easy to reach. It takes some effort to find them because they're hidden along the edges of the marshes, beside quiet sloughs, or down in river plain bottomlands that can be explored only by foot. Established trails usually lead near them but not in every case. Check with U.S. Forest Service officials and have them mark specific directions on maps for you.

The national forests of East Texas offer more than the attraction of big trees, however. The woods are filled with the flitting yellows and grays of warblers, while the forest floor is alive with the greens and lavenders of orchids and other tiny flowers. They, too, are part of the mystique of the big trees.

Hot Spots

In the Big Slough Wilderness of the **Davy Crockett National Forest,** a 3,040-acre tract located approximately 16 miles east of Crockett, both the state champion loblolly pine and the national champion water elm can be found. Although forest service roads will get you close, you'll still have to walk. Contact the forest rangers (1240 East Loop 304, Crockett, TX 75835, (409) 544-2046) for specific directions.

Four state champion trees, the flatwoods plum, eastern hop-hornbeam, Florida sugar maple, and little-hip hawthorn, as well as the largest American beech and southern magnolia ecosystem in the world are located in the Indian Mounds Wilderness Area of the **Sabine National Forest** just a few miles east of the small city of Hemphill. Again, a combination of forest service roads and walking will be needed. For specific information, contact the ranger station in Hemphill (201 South Palm, Hemphill, TX 75948, (409) 787-3870).

One of the most impressive wilderness areas in East Texas is the Upland Island Wilderness in the **Angelina National Forest.** This 14,200-acre tract was logged heavily around 1900 but has since reestablished itself well. State champion trees include a 165-foot cherrybark oak, the tallest of all champion trees east of the Rockies, and a shagbark hickory, as well as the national champion barberry hawthorn, Florida basswood, and snow-bell tree.

The national champion longleaf pine, 125 feet tall and approximately 380 years old, which also grew here, was blown down by a storm in 1989, but a number of 500-year-old bald cypress trees are still standing. This amazing diversity isn't limited to trees, either. Scientists from nearby Stephen F. Austin University have identified more than 450 different species of plants here, including six orchids.

Upland Island Wilderness is located approximately 10 miles east of the town of Zavalla just off TX Hwy 63. For specific directions on how to reach any of the champion trees, contact the Angelina National Forest (P.O. Box 756, Lufkin, TX 75901, (409) 639-8501).

The most famous state champion tree and the one most easily viewed is the state champion live oak, located in **Goose Island State Park** north of Rockport. The tree is more than 1,000 years old and measures 35 feet in circumference. To reach this tree, follow TX Hwy 35 north from Rockport for 10 miles and turn east on Park Road 13 to the entrance of Goose Island State Park. Take Palmetto Road north off Park Road 13 and follow the signs.

64

Pelican Watching

A wonderful bird is the pelican,
His bill will hold more than his belican.

How many children have learned to recognize the great white pelican through this comical verse by Dixon L. Merrit? Indeed, the number must be incalculable, but what is even more remarkable is that the poem is true: a white pelican's pouch does hold more than its stomach, which makes it one of North America's most interesting birds.

It certainly is one of the largest, with a wingspan often approaching nine feet and a weight of up to 15 pounds. On land, these birds aren't the most agile of creatures, often walking with a side-to-side wobble that makes one wonder if they know what their feet are for.

But in the water or in the air, the white pelican is a picture of dignity. They float like corks and swim with strong powerful strokes. In the cool breezes of November, they can soar like hawks, circling higher and higher to find just the right wind and then setting sail with their slow, deliberate wing beats.

Although the white pelican is closely related to the brown pelican, the two have distinct differences. Brown pelicans are strictly saltwater birds, but white pelicans are found along the coast as well as on the inland lakes. And while the brown pelican is a solitary hunter that dives into the water to catch its prey, white pelicans often feed in cooperative groups.

The white pelican, which migrates to Texas from its breeding grounds in the northwestern U.S., is one of the few birds completely at home in either fresh or saltwater. Large flocks regularly spend the winter on Falcon Lake far from the Gulf.

Swimming side by side in a tight formation, four or five white pelicans will herd a swarm of minnows or small fish against a shoreline or into a shallow pocket where all can enjoy the bounty. They move with their bills partly submerged and scoop up both water and prey—their bill pouch can hold about three gallons of water—always turning in perfect unison.

In some instances, they'll even flap their wings on the water to frighten the fish in the direction they want them to go. Their primary food is gizzard shad and other small rough fish with little or no commercial or sporting value; crayfish are also eaten occasionally if they happen to get caught in the line of march.

Easily one of the most noticeable features about white pelicans is their calmness. The birds seem to become quite relaxed in the presence of humans and don't move until the last moment. Even then they are not hurried or frantic. In the water, they swim just fast enough to stay out of harm's way and often move back and forth between two chosen points.

The majority of white pelicans nest across the northern United States between the Pacific Northwest and the upper Midwest. Major nesting areas are located in Nevada, Utah, North Dakota, and Montana, and they've probably been using those sites for hundreds and possibly thousands of years. Ornithologists who have studied these birds believe they've been on earth for about 35 million years and have changed very little in that time.

Annual migrations bring them to Texas as early as October, and some remain as late as April. Some stay on freshwater lakes for a couple of weeks before continuing to the coast, and others spend the entire winter in freshwater.

Even though they hardly ever utter a sound, white pelicans are gregarious birds that not only migrate in large flocks but stay in those flocks in their wintering areas. Rarely do you see a white pelican alone, and there are recorded instances of injured or disabled birds being cared for by other members of the flock.

Where to Find Pelicans around Grand Lake

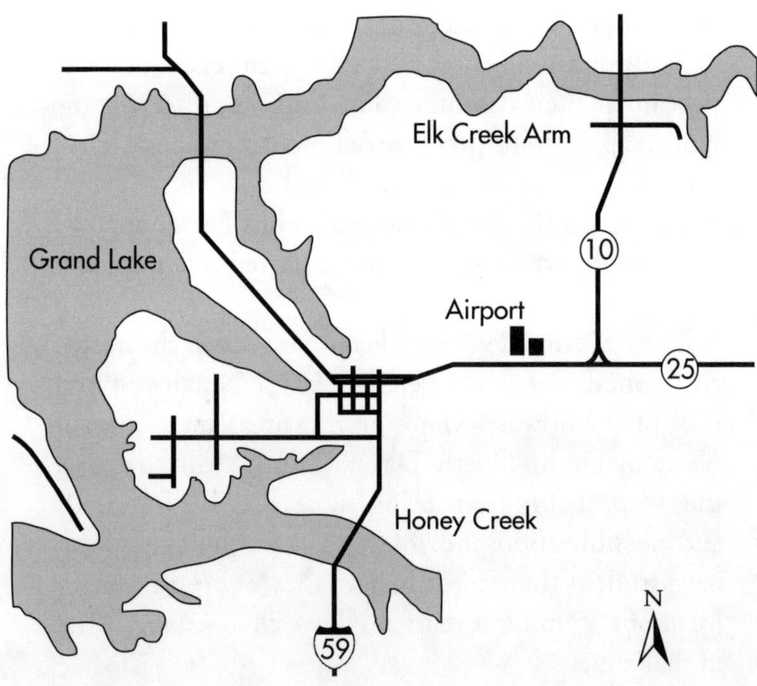

Hot Spots

One of the largest concentrations of white pelicans gather each winter on Falcon Reservoir, a 78,000-acre impoundment on the Rio Grande approximately 75 miles south of Laredo. The best place to see them is from **Falcon State Park;** follow U.S. Hwy 83 south from Zapata for 32 miles, then turn right on FM 2098. Follow this 4 miles to Falcon Heights; at the four-way stop sign turn right and follow this road 1 mile to the park. Signs point the way.

White pelicans also winter at **Hagerman National Wildlife Refuge** near Sherman. To reach the refuge, follow U.S. Hwy 82 west to FM 1417, then go north approximately 5 miles to the refuge road. Signs point the way. Several narrow peninsulas extend into the lake from the main refuge road; all are open to vehicles to allow a closer view of the wildlife.

Along the coast, one of the favorite pelican viewing areas is at **San Luis Pass** on the west end of Galveston Island. Take FM 3005 (also known as Beach Road) south out of Galveston approximately 20 miles to the bridge that crosses the pass. Instead of crossing the bridge, however, park on the side of the road and walk to the bay side of the island. Both white and brown pelicans inhabit much of this section of protected coastline, as do a variety of shorebirds.

In Oklahoma, migrating white pelicans stop for several weeks in September and October on **Grand Lake** of the Cherokees near Grove and Bernice. Look for them first on the northern end of the lake around the Twin Bridges area near Wyandotte.

Other spots include both sides of Sailboat Bridge; in Wolf Creek near City Park at 16th Street; and in Carey Bay.

65

November Shorttakes

Carmen Deer

November is an excellent time to observe one of the smallest and least-known subspecies of whitetail deer, the Sierra del Carmen whitetail *(Odovoileus virginianus carminis),* which is found only in the Chisos Mountains of **Big Bend National Park** and the adjoining Sierra del Carmen Mountains of Mexico. It represents a living example of biological isolation caused by climate and terrain changes over tens of thousands of years.

The animals seldom venture below 5,000 feet, but they can be seen by hiking some of the trails that lead from Panther Junction into the higher elevations of oak and conifer. Deer are also frequently seen while driving along the steep, climbing road from park headquarters to the Chisos Basin campgrounds and lodge. This 12-mile route is well marked, and wildlife is most frequently observed during the early morning and late afternoon hours.

Hikers and backpackers see the diminutive deer along the Lost Mine Trail (5 miles round trip); Emory Peak Trail (9 miles round trip); and South Rim Trail (14 miles round trip). These trails all begin in or near the basin and climb into the mountains. Both the South Rim and Emory Peak Trails are long and arduous and should be attempted only by those in very good physical condition.

Complete information on the current conditions of each trail, water availability, and backcountry use permits is available by contacting the Superintendent, Big Bend National Park, Big Bend National Park, TX 79834, (915) 477-2251.

66

A Closer Look: Tumbleweeds

Anyone who has ever watched a western movie, especially one made more than a decade ago and featuring a ghost town, has probably noticed a strange, basketball-shaped plant rolling across the screen at some point during the show. It was a tumbleweed, which in Hollywood terms at least, has come to symbolize wind, desolation, and harshness in the West.

Hollywood is mostly wrong but partially right. There really is a tumbleweed, and they are seen most often in the winter wind as they roll and bounce across the landscape. Although tumbleweeds grow in desolate places, they also do well in fairly crowded country, and it isn't always the harshest terrain, either.

The real tumbleweed *(Salssola kali)* is actually an annual plant known as the Russian thistle. It is not a true thistle, but rather an herb that is believed to have been accidentally introduced from Europe sometime during the mid- to late ninteenth century. Botanists speculate that the plant's seeds were included with a shipment of produce, since tumbleweeds frequently grow adjacent to cultivated fields.

Tumbleweeds are unusual plants in that they don't become "woody" until they mature. They are herbaceous but do not have an obvious leaf structure, either. When it begins growing, the tumbleweed is green to greenish gold and shaped somewhat like a conifer in that it spreads at the base and grows to a point, sometimes as much as four feet tall. It has a very shallow root system and does not require much water. Overall, it can be found from Texas to California and north to the Canadian border across Montana and North Dakota.

Although not a true thistle, the tumbleweed does have some characteristics of a thistle in that its branches feel slightly thorny or sharp to the touch. Anyone walking through a field of growing tumbleweeds and brushing against them will definitely feel them. Perhaps this is the reason that cattle won't eat them.

The very young green plants supposedly are edible, however. They can be boiled in water and butter like asparagus and eaten with no ill effects; they are bland and tasteless. In his interesting book *The History and Folklore of North American Wildflowers,* author Timothy Coffee writes that the Zuni Indians of the American Southwest ate tumbleweed seeds raw and then later ground them with cornmeal, added water to the mixture, and steamed them.

While it makes a good legend, there is some question about whether the Zuni were actually eating tumbleweed seeds or those of another similar plant. Coffee places tumbleweed in the amaranth family *(Amaranthus blitoides),* which includes some 800 species of herbs and shrubs, but many botanists today disagree.

Tumbleweeds flower during the summer, but the blossoms are insignificant because of their small size. Seeds probably start appearing around October as the plant's branches begin to harden. This drying and hardening process is partially what gives the tumbleweed its more rounded shape. Tumbling probably also contributes to its shape.

In the winter, the tumbleweed dies, and when strong winds begin blowing, as they always do across western and northern Texas, the plant usually snaps at ground level and begins its tumbling, bouncing journey. As it bounces, it disperses its seeds along the way, insuring another generation of tumbleweeds for the coming year. One reason tumbleweeds are found so often around the edges of cultivated fields is that many get snagged on fencelines and simply drop their seeds on the spot.

A few years ago, according to Denny Miller of the Chihuahuan Desert Visitor Center and Research Institute in Alpine, efforts were undertaken to find an economic use for tumbleweeds. Dried plants were compressed into briquets as a possible alternative to charcoal, as they apparently burn with a very high BTU rating. The research was eventually dropped for a variety of reasons.

Today, the only real value of tumbleweeds is ornamental. In West Texas, some collect the dried weeds, spray-paint them white, and stack them atop each other like a snowman. Others collect smaller tumbleweeds and place them among larger potted plants and indoor trees.

Of course, Hollywood likes them just the way they are, following the wind across field and prairie canyon. In this regard, tumbleweeds certainly are a symbol of the Old West, but they're alive and well today, too.

December

Notes

67

The Odyssey of the Whooping Cranes

Each autumn they begin to arrive—singularly, in twos and threes, and occasionally in small groups—until perhaps finally as many as 150 birds, nearly the world's entire wild population, will be present. Their nesting success in the Northwest Territories of Canada has been recorded, their feeding stopover in Saskatchewan documented, and their migration across six states tracked by a small army of biologists and ornithologists.

The wintering birds, of course, are the whooping cranes, and their 2,600-mile journey from Wood Buffalo National Park just south of Great Slave Lake is so closely monitored that their arrival time at Aransas National Wildlife Refuge on the Texas Gulf Coast can practically be calculated within hours. That's because the whooping crane, more than any other species of bird, mammal, or reptile in the United States, has come to symbolize the successful recovery of an endangered species.

Although these regal white birds, which may stand as tall as five feet and have a seven-foot wingspan, are not out of danger, they have made a remarkable comeback in the last half-century. In 1944, only 21 whoopers were known to exist in the wild; during the winter of 1995-96, 158 birds were counted at Aransas.

Historically, whooping cranes probably ranged from as far north as their present nesting grounds in Canada all the way to Mexico, and eastward across most of the United States. Thousands originally wintered along the Gulf Coast into Louisiana, and some even remained there year-round.

Between about 1850 and 1920, however, the birds were nearly wiped out by both hunters and habitat loss. Only the creation of the Aransas National Wildlife Refuge in 1937, one of their original wintering grounds, saved the whooping cranes from extinction.

Few birds inspire as much awe at first glimpse as do the whoopers. With their large size and white plumage, they are clearly visible for half a mile or more across the salt marsh. Their long legs make giant strides along the water's edge, and in flight their wide, black-tipped wings seem to flap in slow motion.

Whooping cranes mate for life, and not only do they fly together as a family group, but they often establish the same feeding area at Aransas year after year. This territory may be as much as 300 acres, and when the young pair off at three to five years of age, they tend to establish their own feeding grounds near that of their parents.

There seems to be little that whooping cranes won't eat. Minnows, snails, small snakes, clams, crabs, worms, crayfish, insects, acorns, and marsh greenery are all on the menu. Surprisingly, the birds are not particularly good at fishing as are the smaller herons and egrets, and in years when the natural bounty of the refuge is slim, the birds are fed a supplement of grain and corn.

Each year between 125 and 150 whooping cranes migrate from the Northwest Territories to the Aransas National Wildlife Refuge. Pairs claim their feeding areas, often the same spots year after year, and remain on the refuge until April.

The whoopers remain in Texas until about mid-April, then leave as they arrived, individually or in small groups. The trip back to the Northwest Territories takes about three weeks, including stops for food and bad weather.

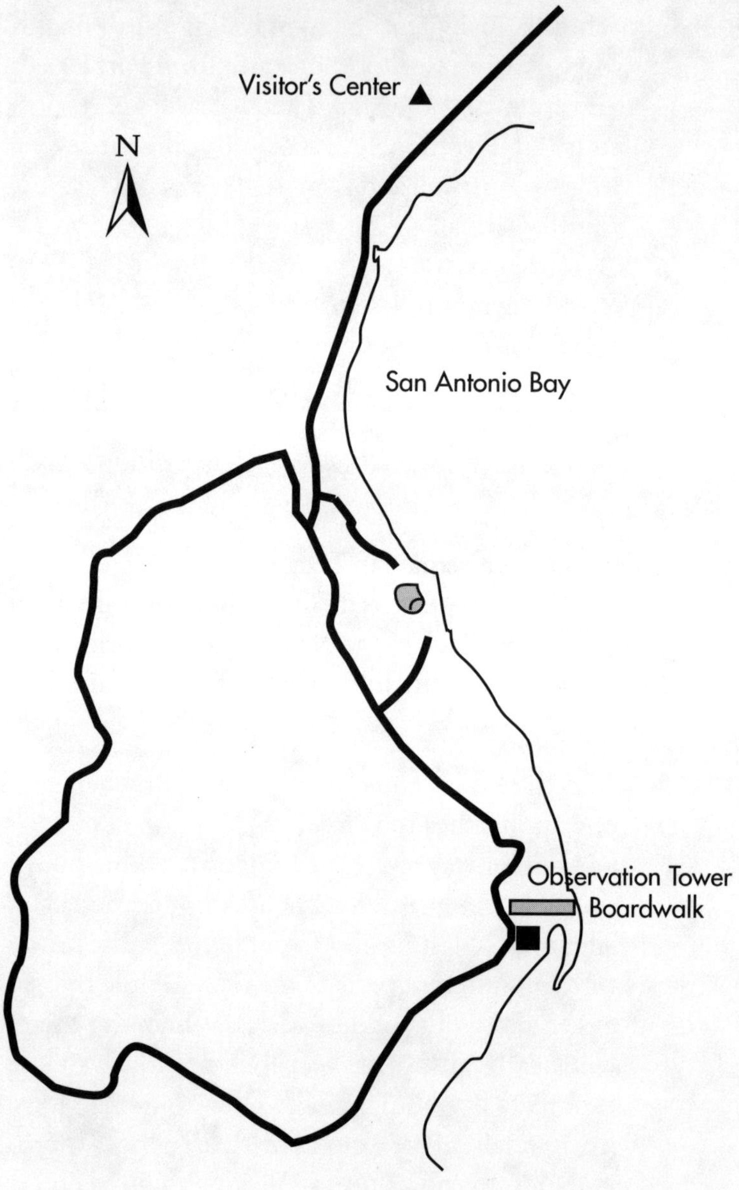
Aransas National Wildlife Refuge
Public Use Area
Visitor's Center
N
San Antonio Bay
Observation Tower
Boardwalk

Hot Spots

Aransas National Wildlife Refuge near the city of Rockport is the most reliable place in the United States to see the whooping cranes. The refuge is easily reached by traveling north on TX Hwy 35 from Rockport or south from Port Lavaca and following the signs. You'll leave TX 35 just south of Tivoli on FM 239 and follow it several miles to Austwell and then to the refuge. The route is well marked.

Your first stop at the refuge should be at the Visitor Center, where sign in is required. Here you can see an exhibit of the cranes, as well as receive up-to-date sighting information. You will also be cautioned not to frighten or harass the cranes in any manner, for to do so is a federal offense.

From there, follow the paved road to the Observation Tower overlooking Mustang Lake. Occasionally, you'll see a pair of whoopers feeding on the tidal flat at the edge of the water. You can follow the boardwalk across the tidal flat, but don't expect the birds to stand and pose for you; even though 75,000 people a year visit Aransas, the cranes are wary and quickly take flight when anyone approaches too close.

Another way to see the birds is by taking one of the boat tours offered by area concessionaires. These tours, lasting about four hours, cruise slowly through different parts of the refuge while trained guides point out various species. Whooping cranes will nearly always be seen but not always close enough to be photographed. These tour boats leave Rockport and Port Aransas marinas for both morning and afternoon tours. Although you'll almost certainly want to take your own binoculars, powerful spotting scopes are usually provided.

Be sure to dress warmly, because you'll spend most of your time on the upper deck in the cold winter air. Tour costs are approximately $25 per person, and you need to purchase your ticket early because the boats are often crowded, frequently with bird-watching enthusiasts from many different states.

A third option to see the whooping cranes, which usually appeals to more serious photographers, involves chartering your own guide boat. Using a small runabout that will hold up to four passengers, a knowledgeable guide will take you much closer to the whooping cranes, sometimes within a few yards, and remain there as long as you wish. The cost for this trip is $35/hour, with a four-hour minimum, and reservations must be made in advance.

Boat tour operators include Capt. Ted's Whooping Crane Tours in Rockport (512-729-9589); and Fisherman's Wharf in Port Aransas (512-749-5760).

While whooping cranes are the main attraction for most Aransas visitors, don't overlook the other wildlife here. Nearly 400 species of birds have been identified at this refuge, the highest bird count in the entire national wildlife refuge system. Among them are two dozen species of ducks, 15 species of hawks, 6 species of herons, and nearly three dozen species of warblers.

You'll see four-legged residents, as well, including whitetail deer, javelina, and even alligators.

Many of them can be spotted by taking the 16-mile auto loop tour through the refuge, or by walking one of the four hiking trails leading through the different marsh and upland habitats.

The refuge is open during the daylight hours year-round; no overnight camping is permitted. The headquarters office can be reached by writing Aransas NWR, P.O. Box 100, Austwell, TX 77950, or by telephone at (512) 286-3559.

68

Christmas Bird Counts

They arrive the evening before to meet new friends, receive team assignments, and find a place to spread their sleeping bags. At dawn the next morning, they're out with binoculars, bird books, and note pads recording each and every bird they see. They're participating in what has become one of the most important wildlife census gatherings in the world, the annual Audubon Society Christmas Bird Count. In 1995, more than 44,000 volunteers participated in about 1,700 separate counts not only throughout the United States but also in Canada, Central and South America, and the West Indies.

That's quite a difference from the 27 conservationists who participated in the first count, held Christmas Day 1900 in Englewood, New Jersey. The count was organized by Frank Chapman as a protest to the annual "side hunt" in which teams competed to see how many birds they could shoot.

Today, the importance of the counts cannot be overestimated. The information collected becomes part of an overall census of populations of different species. Because birds are a barometer of environmental and ecological conditions nationwide, a year-to-year decline in a species indicates a problem in the environment. Christmas counts, for example, helped confirm the decline of the bald eagle due to pesticide contamination.

The individual counts take place in a 24-hour calendar day during a two-to-three-week period in late December and early January. They are sponsored jointly by the National Audubon Society and the U.S. Fish and Wildlife Service, and anyone can participate, regardless of expertise in identifying birds. Counts are conducted by various organizations including not only local Audubon Society chapters, but also the Nature Conservancy and others.

Each count group is assigned a circle 15 miles in diameter, an area of more than 175 square miles. Teams of two or three individual counters are given a specific sector to cover within this circle. Counts may be made by automobile, on foot, by boat, and even from the air. While a full 24-hour period is open for the count, most spend from dawn to dusk in the field. Due to work requirements, some counters must limit their time to before or after office hours; there are no specific rules as to how long an individual must stay out. Statistics collected by each count are sent to the National Audubon Society and later published in the society's *American Birds* magazine.

The fun and popularity of the bird counts has led to friendly competitions between different parts of the nation to see who counts the highest number of species. The Texas coast always places very high, and in 1994 Corpus Christi counters recorded the most species anywhere in the United States: 213.

Individuals may participate in as many counts as they wish and are not limited to their own geographical region. The cost is only $5 per person, which goes to the

Each winter in December and early January, thousands of observers go afield as part of the annual Audubon Bird Counts. Texas consistently produces some of the highest counts in the nation; egrets like this are a common sight.

National Audubon Society, and all that's required is a telephone call or letter to a regional Audubon office to make a reservation.

Hot Spots

To participate in a Christmas Bird Count in Texas, volunteers may contact the **National Audubon Society Southwest Regional Office** at 2525 Wallingwood, Suite 301, Austin, TX 78746, (512) 327-1943, and request a list of chapters conducting counts.

Among the most popular is the count in the Freeport area along the coast near Houston. For specific information on this count, contact the **Houston Audubon Society,** 440 Wilchester, Houston, TX 77079, (713) 932-1639. The Corpus Christi count is also extremely popular. For information contact the **Coastal Bend Audubon Society,** 3525 Bluebonnet, Corpus Christi, TX 78408, (512) 882-7232.

Another count growing in popularity is the one conducted on the **Nature Conservancy's Mad Island Preserve** near the city of Palacios. During their first count in 1993, volunteers here counted 197 different species, a national record for "rookie" counts; in 1994 a total of 205 species were counted, second only to Corpus Christi nationwide. For information on this count, contact the Nature Conservancy/Mad Island, P.O. Box 163, Collegeport, TX 77428, (512) 972-2559.

Some of the highest winter bird counts taken each year are made near the city of Freeport along the Texas Gulf Coast. Great blue herons, common throughout Texas, are always included in the Freeport count.

69

Snow Goose Blizzards

Each winter, the forecast remains the same for portions of the Texas coast: heavy snows. This isn't a weather forecast but a goose forecast, predicting the arrival of more than a million white snow geese to the state. They begin arriving in October and remain until March or April, but December is a good month for viewing.

Snow geese are one of the eight species of geese found in North America and are easily distinguished from the others by their overall white coloration. The tips of the wings (the primary feathers) are black, and the bill is slightly pinkish. The Texas variety is the lesser snow goose; a similarly colored but slightly larger greater snow goose winters along the Atlantic Coast.

Like all geese, the snow goose is both highly gregarious and extremely vocal. The birds nest, migrate, and winter in concentrations that number in the thousands. They're fairly easy to find, too, because they're usually talking to each other.

This is truest in the early light of dawn when the birds wake up at their roosting site and immediately begin honking. This gradually rises to an almost deafening cacophony until suddenly nearly as one an entire flock of perhaps 20,000 or more takes wing and heads toward the daily feeding ground.

The Texas snow geese spend their summers nesting

in the high Arctic from Baffin Island to Siberia. Nests are made near the Arctic Ocean in the flat tundra, and the eggs hatch by early August. The young can fly by October, which is just in time to begin the long migration south. When full grown, they'll have a wingspan of nearly five feet and a flight speed of more than 50 miles per hour.

The geese have been migrating south for centuries, and in recent years their numbers have generally stabilized at between 750,000 and one million birds. They are heavily hunted in several areas; in fact, the snow goose harvest is higher than that of any other ducks or geese. Commercial goose hunting had its start in Texas in the early 1950s and today is so popular that hunters come from around the nation. The hunting is very well controlled on both private and federal lands and has had little if any detrimental effect on snow goose populations. At the same time, the popularity of goose hunting has greatly aided the economies of several cities and provided hundreds of related jobs.

Each winter, tens of thousands of lesser snow geese migrate to Texas, with the largest concentrations occurring just a short driving distance from Houston.

Hot Spots

The best place to see snow geese is the **Katy Prairie,** the name given to the vast, flat rice fields west of Houston. The specific viewing areas will change from week to week as the birds move to different feeding areas, but a good place to make your headquarters is **Eagle Lake,** located approximately 60 miles west of Houston on U.S. Alt. 90. From Eagle Lake you can easily go in several directions, depending on where the geese are.

Your first drive should be along FM 3013 north toward Sealy, where you start looking for the birds on either side of the road in the fields. Another choice is to follow FM 102 south from Eagle Lake and turn right on FM 950. Follow this to TX Hwy 71 and turn right (north) toward the town of Altair. Flocks of geese can be anywhere along these roads.

Still another option is to turn left (south) on TX 71 and head toward the city of El Campo. Before reaching El Campo, turn left (east) on FM 961. You can follow this all the way to U.S. Hwy 59 near the city of Wharton, or turn right on FM 960, which will take you to the outskirts of El Campo on U.S. 59. If you turn left onto FM 960, it will take you to FM 102, which will lead you back to Eagle Lake.

It is also possible to book a trip with one of the numerous hunting outfitters in this area, even though you may be shooting with only a camera. A list of outfitters is available from the Eagle Lake Chamber of Commerce, 408 East Main, Eagle Lake, TX 77434, (409) 234-2780.

Spectacular viewing opportunities also exist at **San Bernard National Wildlife Refuge** south of Wharton. From Wharton follow TX Hwy 60 south to Bay City, turn left (east) on TX Hwy 35 and follow this 24 miles to West Columbia. Turn south on TX Hwy 36 and follow this south through Brazoria to FM 2611. Turn right (southeast) on FM 2611 and follow it 4 miles to FM 2918. Turn left (south) on FM 2918 and follow the signs to the entrance. Practically any tour road may present good views of geese.

Brazoria National Wildlife Refuge also offers excellent sighting opportunities for snow geese, particularly near Teal and Rogers ponds, which are accessible along the $7^1/_2$-mile Big Slough auto tour. This refuge is more primitive and has no visitor center or on-site personnel; it is open only on the first full weekend of each month all year and the third weekend between November and May. Someone will open the gate for visitors, however, if prior arrangements are made by telephone.

To reach Brazoria NWR, follow FM 523 south from Angleton to FM 227; turn left on FM 227 and follow it to the entrance. For the most up-to-date information about snow goose populations on either refuge, contact Brazoria National Wildlife Refuge Complex, 1212 North Velasco, Suite 200, Angleton, TX 77516, (409) 849-6062.

Thousands of snow geese also concentrate at **Anahuac National Wildlife Refuge** east of Houston. To reach the refuge, follow I-10 east from Houston approximately 50 miles to TX Hwy 61. Turn south on TX 61 for 2 miles to FM 562. Follow FM 562 south for 8 miles, then turn left (east) on FM 1985 and follow this 4 miles to the refuge. Additional information is available by contacting the refuge at P.O. Box 278, Anahuac, TX 77514, (409) 839-2680.

70

The Deer with Big Ears

For those accustomed to seeing the elegant and stately whitetail deer, the first encounter with its close cousin, the mule deer, is often surprising, for the two have distinctly different personalities. While the whitetail is generally small, nervous, and quick to run, the mule deer is heavier, far more curious, and frequently hops as if on a pogo stick.

Mule deer are also far less numerous throughout their entire range, which extends from the western Canadian provinces southward into Mexico. There are 11 subspecies of mule deer; the animal inhabiting the rough, dry desert country of western Texas is the subspecies *Odocoileus hemionus crooki,* or desert mule deer.

All mule deer species are somewhat similar in appearance, with gray to brown hair, a black-tipped tail, and bifurcated or forked antlers. They also have unusually large ears, from which their name is derived. *Odocoileus* comes from the Greek word meaning "mule," another well-known animal with larger than normal ears.

When a mule deer is curious, which seems to be much of the time, the ears extend straight out from the head, as if tuned like satellite dishes. There is no question that hearing and smell are the mule deer's keenest senses, but researchers don't believe the big ears necessarily help a mule deer hear any better than a whitetail does with its smaller ears.

Mule deer are easily identified by their large, mulelike ears. They are not nearly as numerous in Texas as whitetails; however, they can be viewed in Davis Mountains State Park.

What makes a mule deer's ears so noticeable is the fact that an observer gets to see them so clearly, for this is an animal that sometimes seems glued to the ground by curiosity. It will stand and watch and listen to something it can't quite understand much longer than any whitetail ever will, and when it finally does flee, it may go only a few yards before it stops to stare and listen again. This initial movement is often a series of hops or bounds, in which the animal springs into the air, lands on all four feet, then springs again. Although most hops cover only four or five feet, some mule deer have been seen to broad jump more than 20 feet in a single leap. The animal won't raise its tail in alarm the way whitetails do, nor does it tend to snort like alarmed whitetails do. It simply leaves.

When a mule deer finally decides it has seen or heard enough, the hopping ends and the running begins. Although it probably won't head into the next county, it will easily put some distance between itself and whatever frightened it. Then, often in plain view, it will stop once more to look back, stick out those big ears again, and try to figure out what's happening.

Desert mule deer do not grow quite as large as the more widespread Rocky Mountain mule deer, but that doesn't mean their antlers are any less impressive. Each beam forks and in mature bucks forks a second time, producing a total of 10 points including the two brow tines. Although there may not be as many points, the antlers tend to be higher and wider than those of a whitetail, and more massive. In most of Texas, the antlers are shed by early January.

Looking at the terrain desert mule deer inhabit, one has to wonder how any deer can find enough food to support antler growth, but in truth, the animals do extremely well. Grasses, berries, sage, twigs, and flowers all form part of their diet. The animals especially seem to like various cactus plants, and they aren't bothered in the least by the thorny spines.

Hot Spots

Viewing mule deer in Texas presents a problem similar to that for viewing many other species: The majority of land in the state is privately owned, and trespassers, regardless of their intentions, are not appreciated. There are, however, several public locations where the animals can often be seen fairly reliably. Perhaps the best is **Davis Mountains State Park,** located just north of the city of Fort Davis.

There is only one entrance to the park, off TX 118, and mule deer can often be seen browsing in late afternoon along the steep slope on the right just past the park entrance on Park Road 3. Continue along this paved drive and turn left on the first paved road leading into the campground. Mule deer frequently come down out of the surrounding hills and simply wander through the entire campground. This can happen at anytime during the day, so ask park rangers about deer sightings when you check in.

Mule deer are also often spotted along **TX Highway 118 North** between the city of Fort Davis and the park entrance. Once you pass the old military fort, look for deer along the left at the foot of the rocky hillsides.

Another place to view mule deer is in **Guadalupe Mountains National Park,** particularly in late afternoon, as they come to various watering holes in the thick brush not far from Pine Springs Campground and the Frijole Visitor Center. Occasionally, mule deer can be seen in the brush while driving along U.S. Hwy 62/180, which leads through a corner of the park.

Mule deer can also be seen in **Big Bend National Park,** usually within a mile of the headquarters at Panther Junction. Small herds often feed along the road leading to Rio Grande Village, as well as near mile marker 1 on both sides of the road leading to Persimmon Gap.

Two places in the Panhandle offer excellent mule deer viewing, Caprock Canyons State Park near Quitaque and Buffalo Lake National Wildlife Refuge near Canyon. In **Caprock Canyons State Park,** look for mule deer anywhere along the paved park road, but especially near bridge crossings of the South Prong of Little Red River, or when hiking near the North Prong Primitive Camping Area.

To reach **Buffalo Lake National Wildlife Refuge,** follow FM 168 south from Umbarger 3 miles and turn right at the refuge entrance sign. After registering, continue along the 5-mile interpretive auto driving tour and look for mule deer, particularly in early morning, near the campground as well as the edges of the cedar thickets.

71

December Shorttakes

Chachalaca

In the entire United States the chachalaca (CHA-cha-LAH-kah) is found only in a few scattered locations in the lower Rio Grande Valley. This bird is somewhat chickenlike in appearance and size, except that it has a long tail and its overall coloration is brown and gray. Another difference is that its toe configuration allows it to walk on tree limbs and branches as easily as on the ground; chachalacas will often walk through the upper branches of the forest rather than flying from place to place. The bird's name comes from its wild, loud, bawdy cry, "Cha-cha-lak, cha-cha-lak!" heard most often during the early morning and late afternoon hours or, strangely enough, just before a thunderstorm.

Chachalacas are often seen at **Bentsen–Rio Grande Valley State Park** near Mission. Slowly drive down Park Road 43 past the headquarters office and follow it on the big loop around the campgrounds to the Rio Grande Hiking Trail. At **Santa Ana National Wildlife Refuge,** chachalacas are frequently seen along any of the three walking trails, particularly the short paved path leading out from refuge headquarters.

72

A Closer Look: Endangered Species

When Christopher Columbus first set foot in the New World that October day in 1492, he inadvertently set into motion a cycle of competition so complex that even the best scientific minds of today have trouble understanding it. The cycle he started is the competition for space between human beings and nature, and thus far, human beings have won most of it.

The result since that day has been the total extinction of more than 500 species of plants, mammals, and fish. Nearly 1,000 more are officially threatened with extinction and form what is known as the Endangered Species List. First compiled in 1973 with the passage of the Federal Endangered Species Act, the list included just 78 species in North America. By 1995 the list had grown to 956; of those, 72 are found in Texas.

That Texas has so many endangered species is not surprising, given the state's distinction as a biological crossroads for several different ecological zones. Texas has been in the forefront of wildlife conservation and protection since 1903, when the state passed its first laws protecting various species of nongame birds from hunting. Hunting licenses were mandated in 1907, and by 1910 the state had hired its first game wardens.

In 1970, Texas initiated special research and management programs for nongame species and three years later passed its own Endangered Species Act. The term "endangered" refers to those plants, mammals, fish, and invertebrates near extinction throughout all or most of their range; the next category, "threatened," designates those species likely to become endangered in the near future.

The Endangered Species Act, or ESA, falls under the jurisdiction of the U.S. Fish and Wildlife Service and the National Marine Fisheries Service. Once these two agencies list a species as endangered, no branch of government can proceed with any project that might harm that species without first consulting the two agencies.

Although losing the fight for living space—habitat loss—is certainly one of the major reasons a species becomes threatened or endangered, it is not the only reason. Another is pollution, most often chemical PCB or mercury poisoning, which becomes more intense as it progresses through the food chain.

This biological magnification starts at the bottom of the food chain with plankton, which absorb the contaminant directly from the water. The plankton isn't harmed by the small amount it absorbs, but when a minnow eats a lot of plankton, its poison dosage increases dramatically. A sunfish eating a lot of minnows gets an even larger dose, and a bigger fish eating the sunfish receives a greater amount. Then an eagle or osprey representing the top of the food chain eats several of the fish and gets the largest poison dosage of all. This, of course, is exactly what happened to bald eagles, brown pelicans, peregrine falcons, and other birds during the mid-1960s.

The effects of the contamination showed up not in the consumer birds but in their offspring. Eggshells were too thin to support embryos, and entire generations of species were lost. The population of brown pelicans along the Texas-Louisiana coast fell from 50,000 to less than 100 in only a few years.

Many ask Why be concerned with problems like this? One of the most important reasons is because scientists have learned to use wildlife as a monitor of environmental conditions worldwide. All birds, mammals, fishes, reptiles, and humans begin life the same way, from a fertilized egg. Contaminants that affect the chromosomes and genes of these lesser species will affect—already have affected—human beings.

The success stories detailing the recovery of eagle, pelican, and falcon populations through the reduction of pesticides and contaminants are well known, so there certainly is much to be encouraged about on that front. Solving the problem of habitat loss to save an endangered species is perhaps more difficult. Biologists have begun to realize it will do little good to save a species, even in captive-breeding programs, if there is no habitat for that species back in the wild. As a result, efforts now are turning toward total habitat or ecosystem management.

For this to work, complete cooperation between private landowners and the scientific community is needed. This is certainly true in Texas, where the majority of the land is privately owned. Will landowners be willing to sacrifice property and possibly income to save an endangered species?

In some instances, the answer has already been positive, as ranchers west of Van Horn have allowed the establishment of bighorn sheep herds on their ranches. Landowners have likewise been instrumental over the

The ocelot is extremely rare in Texas, but occasionally one is observed at the Laguna Atascosa National Wildlife Refuge near Harlingen. The small cat prefers the dense brush habitat of South Texas and northern Mexico.

years in the re-establishment of whitetail deer, wild turkey, and pronghorn populations. As human populations grow, however, and competition between human beings and animals for the same land increases, the choices will undoubtedly become harder, especially since the entire Endangered Species Act is based on the simple principle that every species is entitled to exist for its own sake.

Appendix

National Parks, Forests, and Seashores

Angelina National Forest
P.O. Box 756
Lufkin, TX 75901
(409) 639-8501

Big Bend National Park
Big Bend National Park, TX 79834
(915) 477-2251

Big Thicket National Preserve
3785 Milam
Beaumont, TX 77701
(409) 839-2689

Davy Crockett National Forest
1240 East Loop 304
Crockett, TX 75835
(409) 544-2046

Guadalupe Mountains National Park
HC 60, Box 400
Salt Flat, TX 79847-9400
(915) 828-3351

Lake Meredith National Recreation Area
P.O. Box 1460
Fritch, TX 79036
(806) 857-3151

National Forests in Texas
Homer Garrison Federal Building
701 North First Street
Lufkin, TX 75901
(409) 639-8501

Padre Island National Seashore
9405 South Padre Island Drive
Corpus Christi, TX 78418
(512) 937-2621

Sabine National Forest
201 South Palm
Hemphill, TX 75948
(409) 787-3870

USDA Forest Service
2000 South College
(FM 730 South)
Decatur, TX 76234
(817) 627-5475

USDA Forest Service Southwestern Region
Federal Building
517 Gold Avenue, SW
Albuquerque, NM 87102
(505) 476-3300

National Wildlife Refuges

Anahuac NWR
P.O. Box 278
Anahuac, TX 77514
(409) 839-2680

Aransas NWR
P.O. Box 100
Austwell, TX 77950
(512) 286-3559

Attwater Prairie Chicken NWR
P.O. Box 519
Eagle Lake, TX 77434-0519
(409) 234-3021

Brazoria NWR Complex
1212 North Velasco, Suite 200
Angleton, TX 77516-1088
(409) 849-6062

Buffalo Lake NWR
P.O. Box 179
Umbarger, TX 79091
(806) 499-3382

Hagerman NWR
Rt. 3, Box 123
Sherman, TX 75090-9564
(903) 786-2826

Laguna Atascosa NWR
P.O. Box 450

Rio Hondo, TX 78583
(210) 748-3607

McFaddin–Texas Point NWR
P.O. Box 609
Sabine Pass, TX 77655
(409) 971-2909

Muleshoe NWR
P.O. Box 549
Muleshoe, TX 79347
(806) 946-3341

San Bernard NWR
Rt. 1, Box 1335
Brazoria, TX 77422
(409) 964-3639

Santa Ana, Lower Rio Grande Valley NWR Complex
Rt. 2, Box 202A
Room 225
Alamo, TX 78516
(210) 787-3079

Welder Wildlife Foundation
P.O. Box 1400
Sinton, TX 78387
(512) 364-2643

Wichita Mountains NWR
Rt. 1, Box 448
Indiahoma, OK 73552
(405) 429-3221

Texas State Parks

Bastrop State Park
Box 518
Bastrop, TX 78602-0518
(512) 321-2101

Bentsen–Rio Grande Valley State Park
P.O. Box 988
Mission, TX 78573-0988
(210) 585-1107

Big Bend Ranch State Park
HC 70, Box 375
Terlingua, TX 79852
(915) 424-3327

Brazos Bend State Park
21901 FM 762
Needville, TX 77461
(409) 553-5101

Caprock Canyons State Park
P.O. Box 204
Quitaque, TX 79255
(806) 455-1492

Choke Canyon State Park
P.O. Box 1548
Three Rivers, TX 78071
(512) 786-3538

Colorado Bend State Park
Box 118

Bend, TX 76824
(915) 628-3240

Davis Mountains State Park
P.O. Box 1458
Fort Davis, TX 79734
(915) 426-3337

Dinosaur Valley State Park
Box 396
Glen Rose, TX 76043
(817) 897-4588

Fairfield Lake State Park
Rt. 2, Box 912
Fairfield, TX 75840
(903) 389-4514

Falcon State Park
P.O. Box 2
Falcon Heights, TX 78545
(210) 848-5327

Galveston Island State Park
Rt. 4, Box 156A
Galveston, TX 77554
(409) 737-1222

Goose Island State Park
HC 01, Box 105
Rockport, TX 78382
(512) 729-2858

Hill Country State Natural Area
Rt. 1, Box 601
Bandera, TX 78003
(210) 796-4413

Inks Lake State Park
Rt. 2, Box 31
Burnet, TX 78611
(512) 793-2223

Kickapoo Cavern State Park
P.O. Box 705
Brackettville, TX 78832
(210) 563-2342

Lost Maples State Natural Area
HC 01, Box 156
Vanderpool, TX 78885
(210) 966-3413

Martin Creek Lake State Park
Rt. 2, Box 20
Tatum, TX 75691
(903) 836-4336

Martin Dies Jr. State Park
Rt. 4, Box 274
Jasper, TX 75951
(409) 384-5231

Matagorda Island State Park
P.O. Box 117
Port O'Connor, TX 77982
(512) 983-2215

Meridian State Park
Box 188
Meridian, TX 76665
(817) 435-2536

Monahans Sandhills State Park
Box 1738
Monahans, TX 79756
(915) 943-2092

Mustang Island State Park
P.O. Box 326
Port Aransas, TX 78373
(512) 749-5246

Palo Duro Canyon State Park
Rt. 2, Box 285
Canyon, TX 79015
(806) 488-2227

Pedernales Falls State Park
Rt. 1, Box 450
Johnson City, TX 78636
(210) 868-7304

Possum Kingdom State Park
Box 36
Caddo, TX 76429
(817) 549-1803

Sea Rim State Park
P.O. Box 1066
Sabine Pass, TX 77655
(409) 971-2559

South Llano River State Park
HC 15, Box 224
Junction, TX 76849
(915) 446-3994

State Agencies and Private Reserves

Armand Bayou Nature Center
P.O. Box 58828
Houston, TX 77258
(713) 474-2551

Elephant Mountain Wildlife Management Area
Texas Parks and Wildlife Department
HC 65, Box 80
Alpine, TX 79830
(915) 364-2228

Fossil Rim Wildlife Center
Rt. 1, Box 210
Glen Rose, TX 76043
(817) 897-2960

Oklahoma Department of Wildlife Conservation
1801 North Lincoln
Oklahoma City, OK 73152
(405) 521-3851

Tallgrass Prairie Preserve
P.O. Box 458
Pawhuska, OK 74056
(918) 287-4803

Texas Parks and Wildlife Department
4200 Smith School Road
Austin, TX 78744
(512) 389-4800

Welder Wildlife Foundation Refuge
P.O. Box 1400
Sinton, TX 78387
(512) 364-2643

Birding Resources

Coastal Bend Audubon Society
3525 Bluebonnet
Corpus Christi, TX 78408
(512) 882-7232

Houston Audubon Society
440 Wilchester
Houston, TX 77079
(713) 932-1639

National Audubon Society
Southwest Regional Office
2525 Wallingwood, Suite 301
Austin, TX 78746
(512) 327-1943

Nature Conservancy/Mad Island
P.O. Box 163
College Port, TX 77428
(512) 972-2559

Nature Conservancy of Texas
P.O. Box 1440
San Antonio, TX 78295-1440
(210) 224-8774

Texas Ornithological Society
326 Live Oak
Ingram, TX 78025

Other Useful Resources

Bat Conservation International
P.O. Box 162603
Austin, TX 78716
(512) 327-9721

Big Bend Area Travel Association
P.O. Box 401
Alpine, TX 79831
(915) 837-2326

Big Spring Chamber of Commerce
P.O. Box 1391
Big Spring, TX 79721
(915) 263-7641

Corpus Christi Area Convention and Tourist Bureau
P.O. Box 1664
Corpus Christi, TX 78403
(800) 678-6232

Eagle Lake Chamber of Commerce
408 East Main
Eagle Lake, TX 77434
(409) 234-2780

Galveston Island Convention and Visitors Bureau
2106 Seawall Boulevard
Galveston, TX 77550
(409) 763-4311

Kingsville Visitor Center
101 North 3rd, Box 1562
Kingsville, TX 78363
(800) 333-5032

Lubbock Convention and Visitors Bureau
P.O. Box 561
Lubbock, TX 79408
(800) 692-4035

National Wildflower Research Center
4801 La Crosse Avenue
Austin, TX 78739
(512) 292-4100

River Parks Authority
707 South Houston
Tulsa, OK 74127
(918) 596-2001

Rockport-Fulton Area Chamber of Commerce
404 Broadway
Rockport, TX 78382
(800) 242-0071

Wills Point Chamber of Commerce
Box 217
Wills Point, TX 75169
(903) 873-3111

Selected Bibliography

Andrews, Jean. *The Texas Bluebonnet.* Austin, TX: University of Texas Press, 1993.

Bauer, Erwin A. *Deer in Their World.* New York, NY: Outdoor Life Books, 1983.

————. *Horned and Antlered Game.* New York, NY: Outdoor Life Books, 1986.

Bent, Arthur Cleveland. *Life Histories of North American Gulls and Terns.* New York, NY: Dover Publications, 1963.

Bent, Arthur Cleveland. *Life Histories of North American Marsh Birds.* New York, NY: Dover Publications, 1963.

Brandenburg, Jim. *An American Safari.* New York, NY: Walker and Co., 1995.

Brown, Joseph E. *Padre Island.* Tucson, AZ: Southwest Parks and Monuments Association, 1991.

Bunton, Mary Taylor. *A Bride on the Old Chisholm Trail in 1886.* San Antonio, TX: Naylor Company, 1939.

Chadwick, Douglas H. "The Endangered Species Act," *National Geographic,* March 1995.

Coffee, Timothy. *The History and Folklore of North American Wildflowers.* New York, NY: Facts on File Books, 1993.

Crockett, James Underwood. *Trees.* New York, NY: Time-Life Books, 1972.

Cummings, Joe. *Texas Handbook.* Chico, CA: Moon Publications, 1992.

Dalrymple, Byron W. *North American Game Animals.* New York, NY: Crown Publishers, 1978.

Dyes, John C. *Nesting Birds of the Coastal Islands.* Austin, TX: University of Texas Press, 1993.

Elias, Thomas S. *The Complete Trees of North America.* New York, NY: Gramercy Publishing, 1987.

Henshall, James A., Dr. *Book of Black Bass.* Cincinnati, OH: The Robert Clark Company, 1904.

Hiller, Ilo. *Introducing Mammals to Young Naturalists.* College Station, TX: Texas A&M University Press, 1990.

Kutak, Edward A. *Birder's Guide to Texas.* Houston, TX: Gulf Publishing, 1993.

Loughmiller, Campbell and Lynn. *Texas Wildflowers.* Austin, TX: University of Texas Press, 1994.

McAlister, Wayne H. and Martha K. *Guidebook to the Aransas National Wildlife Refuge.* Victoria, TX: Mince Country Press, 1987.

McAlister, Wayne H. and Martha K. *Matagorda Island.* Austin, TX: University of Texas Press, 1993.

Milne, Lorus and Margery. *The Nature of Life.* New York, NY: Crown Publishers, 1972.

Peterson, Roger Tory. *Birds of Texas.* New York, NY: Houghton Mifflin, 1988.

Price, Steve. *Wild Places of the South.* Charlotte, NC: East Woods Press, 1980.

Rabkin, Richard. *Nature in the West.* Holt, Rinehart and Winston, 1981.

Reifsnyder, William E. *Weathering the Wilderness.* San Francisco, CA: Sierra Club Books, 1980.

Riley, Laura and William. *Guide to the National Wildlife Refuges.* Garden City, NY: Anchor Press/ Doubleday, 1979.

Seidensticker, John. *Great Cats.* Emmaus, PA: Rodale Press, 1991.

Spearing, Darwin. *Roadside Geology of Texas.* Missoula, MT: Mountain Press Publishing, 1991.

Terres, John K. *The Audubon Society Encyclopedia of North American Birds.* New York, NY: Alfred A. Knopf, 1982.

Warnock, Barton H. *Wildflowers of the Davis Mountains and the Marathon Basin, Texas.* Alpine, TX: Sul Ross State University, 1977.

Wauer, Roland H. *Naturalist's Big Bend.* College Station, TX: Texas A&M University Press. 1980.

Williams, Lovett E., Jr. *The Book of the Wild Turkey.* Tulsa, OK: Winchester Press, 1981.

Index

About the Author

Steve Price has been a full-time writer and photographer for more than 20 years, specializing in outdoor recreation and travel. Formerly the outdoor editor of *Southern Living* magazine and the south regional editor of *Field & Stream,* he has written more than 2,000 magazine articles for dozens of national publications. His weekly column appears in more than 500 newspapers across the United States and Canada. This is his fourth book. He lives on the northern edge of the Hill Country in Granbury, Texas.